From Green to Tee

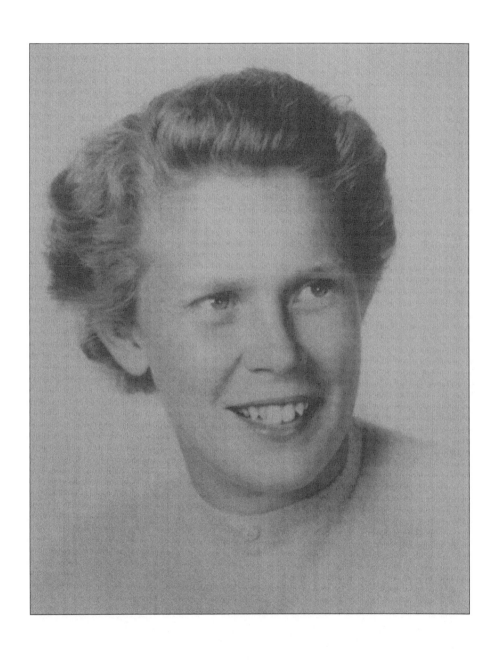

From Green to Tee

SHIRLEY SPORK

with
Nancy Bannon and Connie Kuber

Author's note: References and photos are the sole property of
Shirley Spork from her personal recollection and files.
No part of this publication may be reproduced, or stored in a
retrieval system, or transmitted in any form or by any means,
electronic, mechanical, photocopying, recording, or otherwise,
without written permission of Shirley Spork or her representatives.

All proceeds of this book directly support
junior golf and women's golf programs.

ACKNOWLEDGEMENTS

I do hope you will enjoy my journey through the golfing world. I dedicate this book to all those who love the game: my students, LPGA teachers and coaches, and the LPGA players who I have enjoyed being with on and off the fairways.

First, I want to thank my parents for allowing me to follow my dreams which made all of this possible. The determination to succeed was woven into my life at a very young age.

There are so many people who helped me in the first 20 years of my journey: Otto Hinds, the golf professional who gave me my first used 3, 5, 7, and 9 irons; the Publinx ladies who let me compete with them when I was 13 and 14 years old; Lakepointe and Meadowbrook Country Clubs who allowed me to represent them in the Detroit District and Michigan State competitions; and my college professors who taught me how to teach.

Through my affiliation with Golfcraft, Inc., I was able to travel throughout the United States and Europe giving exhibitions. What an honor that was and what a privilege to meet people all over the world who shared their love for golf.

Becoming a founding member of both the LPGA Tour and LPGA Teaching Division were highlights along the road.

I believe most of my professional success was possible because of my lifelong friendship with a true mentor, Joey Rey. Joey was a PGA Professional at Pasatiempo Golf Club in Santa Cruz, California. I met him in 1951 when I was giving an exhibition at his club. He made it possible for me to secure my first head pro position at the Ukiah Municipal Golf Course. When I questioned whether or not I could handle the job, Joey told me, "You can do it!" I've applied those four powerful words to every challenge I've met along the way.

My second mentor was Ellen Griffin. During my seven-year stint with the National Golf Foundation (NGF) teaching, coaching, and growing the game, she convinced me not to give up trying to start a teaching division within the LPGA.

I also owe a huge debt to the thousands of students who, over the past seven decades, believed in my teaching methodology. I am blessed that so many have become lifelong friends.

And last, but not least, a BIG thank you to Nancy Bannon and Connie Kuber for recording my memories of the past through these fun stories.

All the proceeds from my book will be distributed to several junior golf and women's collegiate golf programs. This wonderful game and the people I've met along the way have given so much to me, and it is a pleasure to pay it forward.

My journey reminds me of a sticker we had in our motorhome . . . "Been There – Done That." So true! I certainly have been blessed to see and do a lot in my life. A great big thank you to all who support this great game we call golf. I hope you enjoy the read.

TABLE OF CONTENTS

HOLE # 1

Began with a Putter

Shirley's childhood was marked by the Great Depression, the Dust Bowl, and World War II. With the economic difficulties of that era, jobs were lost, and new ones were hard to come by. People learned to take care of what they had and make do with just the basics. Rationing was mandated to help the war effort. Everyday life revolved around doing whatever work could be found and trying to merely survive. This was the world which shaped Shirley's work ethic and fighting spirit. What was a little red-haired girl to do? Who knew how green grass, the taunting of a few neighborhood boys, and a special putter would launch a lifetime love affair with the game of golf?

We lived in the city before I got into golf. My mother worked in an office for a men's clothing store that later branched out into a small department store, across the street from the Cadillac Hotel in downtown Detroit.

My grandmother stayed with us and lived to the ripe old age of 90. She believed her longevity was due to the jigger of Manischewitz wine she sipped every night at bedtime.

There wasn't a park or schoolyard near our house. During the summer when my mother had a day off, we would ride the bus to the closest park which was miles away. There, I could rent a bike for a quarter and ride around. We would take our lunch and have a picnic, then go home on the bus. That was our entertainment. In the winter, we would go ice skating at the park.

My father was an electrical engineer for Great Lakes Engineering. The company built freighters that carried iron ore from the Upper Peninsula to the Ford Motor Company foundries. He designed the wiring for the ships. When a ship was launched, we got to go and watch, which didn't happen very often because they were so big and took a long time to build. When they launched ships, they would always launch them sideways.

I had no siblings — only a stillborn sister. My middle name is Geraldine because my mother wanted a boy to call Gerry. It was the era of "Shirleys," like Shirley Temple, which is why they named me Shirley. Shirley is actually a man's name in the English culture. During my golf career, I often got letters addressed to "Mr. Shirley Spork."

In 1939 when I was 12, we moved to the house on the 17th hole of the Bonnie Brook Golf Course. Bonnie Brook opened in 1925. I heard they closed in 2001 to build a Kmart. My father was out of work and had been hired as the caretaker of this property; so we could live there for free.

My mother got a job as a sales clerk and pharmacist's assistant for a druggist at Cunningham's Drug Store, a chain based in Detroit. She would walk to work and in the winter, get frostbitten from the bitter cold. Cunningham's was the largest drug store chain in Michigan but later sold off many of their stores. Their last five stores were bought out by Walgreens.

Our place was in the country on the very northwest corner of Telegraph and 8 Mile Road. It was probably around 15 acres. The house was at the top of the hill, and there was a creek that ran the length of the property. The golf course was just on the other side of the creek. The creek was wide enough that when a golfer sliced their ball over the water and onto our property, it became mine.

Living next to the hilly golf course was perfect for my five-foot long toboggan in the wintertime. The kids in the neighborhood would come down the street to our property. We would cross the creek onto the golf course, walk up the hill, put the toboggan down, and off we went.

One time there was a tremendous snowstorm during the night. The wind blew and made some huge drifts on one of the hills which we didn't know had happened. We got on my toboggan, started down and — whoosh — up in the air we went and came down hard — crunch — landing on each other and banging heads. We were screaming and yelling, and by the time we stopped, some of us had bitten our tongues. But, like most kids, we couldn't wait to race up the hill again. We were so excited because we could make steps out of the drifts to climb to the top. We spent the whole morning trudging up and then flying through the air as we bounced down the hill.

The next day we decided to build a ski jump. My skiing abilities were never going to be good enough for the Olympics; I'll tell you that! But I skied down the golf course hill and flew off of our 20-foot jump. I had received a pair of L.A. Young skis as a gift. L.A. Young was a Detroit company that also made Walter Hagen golf clubs. Hagen was a world-renowned golf professional who was from Traverse City, Michigan.

In the winter months, I would shovel snow off the ice-covered creek which ran into the Rouge River near our house. I also cleared a section of the river off for the boys in the neighborhood and myself to play ice hockey. The creek wasn't wide enough for a hockey game. I owned a hockey puck, so I got to choose the position I wanted to play. If we weren't on the hill with our toboggans or our skis, we were ice skating or playing hockey on the river.

We built bonfires and roasted potatoes, getting them nice and brown. Someone would sneak a quarter-pound of butter from their mother's refrigerator, and we would gnaw on an old baked potato as we dried out our gloves by the fire.

Once I was walking on the ice-covered Rouge River and saw a small open area ahead that wasn't frozen. A little voice in the back of my head said, "Go back, go back," but I didn't listen. I took one more step, and I fell through the ice. Luckily, I bounced up from the bottom right back into the open hole I had made when I fell through. I continued bouncing and breaking the ice until I reached the shore. Painfully I hiked back up the hill to the house with icicles hanging on me, thankful to still be alive.

I played in our little creek which flooded in the springtime. Once, I saw a square, tin container floating along. It must have been from someone's fish pond upstream. I was trying to get it out when suddenly I was sucked into the current. I was swiftly being carried away toward the Rouge River, but luckily my father was home. He was out in the yard at the top of the hill. He heard me crying for help and came running with a rope, threw it out, and pulled me to shore.

We were able to play all summer and all winter right there in my backyard for free! Those were wonderful days. So different from how kids grow up today.

My dad's name was William Spork. My mother called him Billy. I called him Daddy. In the summer we grew a big garden which was about the size of an acre. We had a root cellar underneath the house to store all our vegetables including potatoes for the winter. The garden crop was shared with neighbors. Some of the people we had lived next to in the city would also come out to get our produce and a free fried chicken dinner from Martha and Billy Spork.

We had a picnic table out in the yard where we worked and visited. We canned most of what we picked on a three-burner kerosene stove in the kitchen.

We had a little coal stove in the living room that kept the house warm in the winter. We had a bedroom, a kitchen, a living room, and a small outhouse. Eventually, we saved enough money to buy a telephone pole so we could get electricity. To get electricity on your land, you had to buy your own pole.

We raised chickens and mallard ducks for eggs and meat. I would chop the chicken's head off and clean it, and my mother would fry it. For years I wouldn't eat chicken. I was so damn tired of fried chicken! I hated it, but now I would love to have some of my mother's chicken, hot out of the iron skillet, fried in Crisco.

When I was in high school, I was taking algebra which I thought was stupid. I was struggling and needed help. There were times I would kill one of our chickens and take it with me as payment for the tutor.

After we had electricity, my mother bought a roaster to bake pies and roasts. The least expensive piece of meat to buy was a pork roast. We had one on Sundays and ate it for several more days. We always had leftovers because my mother cooked excessive amounts at one time. She did that so she wouldn't have to cook every day, especially when she was working. It made sense, but for years I hated leftovers. We also had liver once a week because it, too, was cheap. Since we were Catholic, there was always fish on Fridays.

During World War II and several years after, we had food ration stamps for meat, one for sugar, and one for coffee. You could only buy the quantity allowed for those items that were on the stamps.

In the summer, the boys in the neighborhood caddied at the

golf course. On Mondays, it was open for them to play for free. I wanted to play, too. They said I could play with them if I had a golf club. I didn't own a club, and I couldn't just go ask my parents for money to buy one. So, I would wade into the creek and find lost golf balls hidden under the lily pads. My uncle built a drawbridge so that I could cross the creek to sell the balls back to the golfers playing the course. I also went over to the first hole and waded in that pond looking for golf balls. The golf course owner would see me and chase me off. Once, I got stuck in the mud. It wasn't easy getting out.

I started collecting balls in earnest and sold them back to the golfers as they went by our property on their way to the green. I sold some violets to another golfer, and with that, I had a dollar. My mother gave me 13 cents, and with the dollar I had earned, I was all set. I hopped on the streetcar, rode downtown, and at the age of 12, shopped for my first golf club. It was the summer of 1939.

First, I went to Griswold's Sporting Goods store, but they didn't have anything for a dollar. The man at Griswold's told me to go to the S. S. Kresge dime store. He said they had a barrel with clubs in it for a dollar apiece. So I walked down the street, went inside, found the barrel, and looked at all the clubs. There were tall ones, short ones, wooden ones, and metal ones. I picked out a club that was short and straight and had the number 10 on it. I was so excited and couldn't wait to get back home. When I got close to home, I jumped off the streetcar and walked through the neighborhood, so pleased that I had a club to play golf. Once I found the boys,

I proudly showed them my new club. Snickers turned to full out laughter. They were howling because my beautiful new club was . . . a putter!

I didn't care. I marched out to the tee box, set a ball I had found on a tee, which I had also found, and drove it with my brand new putter. I continued to tee my ball up as I played down the fairway, up the hill, and then putted it into the cup. That's how I started playing golf.

I would sneak onto the hole that ran in front of our property — hole #17. I played up 17 and down 18 over and over with my putter until the ranger would see me and chase me off.

In those days when golfers checked in, they bought a ticket. These tickets were punched on the front nine and again as you teed off on the back nine. Sometimes a golfer would sneak by and not have their card punched for the back nine. Later they'd give it to me, so I could play and make it look like I had paid.

I finally got tired of being chased off the course and knew I needed to come up with a better way to work on my golf game. Across the street from our house was a huge field. I went over there and designed my own golf hole. I took a scythe and cut down the tall grass. Then I borrowed my father's mower and mowed the grass shorter like a fairway. I dug a pit to simulate a bunker. Then I mowed a circle to look like a green, cut a hole for the cup, and put a stick in it. Before long, it was ready to go. The kids in the neighborhood didn't care about it. I built it myself and played it by myself. I'd hit my ball into the pit and pretend I was in a sand bunker. I'd always finish the hole by putting out. It kept me busy. Golf was something to do, and I still snuck onto the course whenever I could.

After a while, the ranger gave up chasing me off the course. The pro, Otto Hinds, actually gave me some used golf clubs that were turned in by someone who had bought a new set. There was a three, five, seven, and nine iron. The grips were layered — leather, cork, leather, cork, leather, cork. That's the way they were made back then. But the grips were worn and the only thing left was a strip of leather every other inch. The cork was gone. When I gripped it, there wasn't much to hold onto. My grandfather found an old golf bag in an alley, and we cleaned it up. I was set to go.

I was thrilled and excited to learn how to play with these new clubs, so I rode my bicycle down the road to the free golf clinic at the Redford Golf Course. It was sponsored by the *Detroit Free Press* newspaper and held over a period of four weeks. There wasn't a driving range; they just lined us up on one of the fairways to hit balls. The local men pros came and gave free lessons. Well, the first two times I went, the pros just walked up and down the line, gave a little tip and moved on. Each pro told me that I had a bad grip. They didn't say why or tell me how to fix it; just "You have a bad grip." So finally I said, "I've heard I have a bad grip. How do I fix it?"

I always got a blister on my right thumb when I played, and it was because I had a bad grip. My hand would move during the swing which also caused me to slice the ball. One of the pros finally showed me how to fix my grip, and the ball went straight. So I figured right from the beginning — the most important thing was a good grip!

There were some 50 people in a line, and the pros judged who had improved the most in hitting the ball farther and straighter. I got a prize for hitting the ball straight, which was a MacGregor Sporting Goods certificate for $15. So, I took my certificate to the MacGregor warehouse and picked out a club. A brand new club! I bought my first driver for $15. It was a beautiful black club. I wish I still had it because I sure could hit it. Now I had a new driver and a putter, the two pieces of equipment that are very important: one club to start the game and one to finish. So, with a putter, a driver, and these old, awful irons, I was ready to play golf.

Once, I went to visit my other grandmother who lived near a driving range in Indiana. It cost a quarter to hit a bucket of balls, and the pro lent me a club. I went out in the morning when nobody else was around. There were some big old tractor tires with signs on them . . . "50 yards," "100 yards," and so forth. I aimed at the 100 yard one, swung and heard a crash. I looked out from the tee and saw this little house. A guy came running out of it, waving his arms. I thought, "Oh my, what have I done now?" They had placed a piece of glass hanging down in the middle of the tire, and I had hit it! He wasn't mad. He was excited and said that nobody had ever done that. He gave me five dollars as a prize! I went home and showed the five-dollar bill to my grandmother. She didn't believe my story, so I had to take her over there and have the man explain what had happened. I guess I was always target-oriented. I just saw those signs and thought, "I'd better hit them!"

In 1940, I was 13 years old and in the eighth grade. There were seven kids in my class and four rooms of classes — two downstairs, two upstairs. All we studied was reading, writing, and arithmetic. We did not study history or geography. Once a week the boys did industrial arts, and the girls sewed. I would take the sewing home, and my mother would work on it. I didn't even know how to thread the sewing machine!

One thing I learned about myself that year was that I am claustrophobic! The fire escape from the second floor of the school was a chute. There was a hole in the wall to get into it. I didn't want to go in there. Instead, I volunteered for the fire patrol so I could stay and get everybody else out. That way I wouldn't have to go down the chute.

On the school bus, I was the safety patrol to keep everybody in their seats.

That year I had a desk where the top lifted up, and books were stored in its belly. Inside on the lid, I had a picture of Walter Hagen and Patty Berg. Walter lived in Detroit, and I knew he was a golf pro. They talked about him on the radio and wrote about him in the newspaper that my father read. Patty was from Minneapolis, Minnesota. Who knew I would someday meet Patty, and even play golf with her!

I wanted to play golf, but there were more important things

my family needed. Every summer I set up shop on the side of the fairway. I bought five cases of Coke a week. The Coke man, his name was Eric, told me that the owner of Bonnie Brook didn't want him stopping at my house because I was competition for him. I said, "I buy five cases, and he buys 100. I'm his competitor?"

Eric continued to sell to me. My parents would always give him fresh tomatoes and other garden produce when he stopped by. I sold Coke for a dime. It cost 90 cents for a case of 24. I also sold regular pop for a nickel because it was only 60 cents a case. Milky Ways, Three Musketeers, Paydays, and Hershey bars I sold for a nickel each. For five cents, can you believe that? They were bigger than they are today. I saved enough money to buy myself a bicycle and clothes for school.

I couldn't play golf on the weekends because that was when I was busy at my stand on the 17th fairway at Bonnie Brook selling pop, candy, and the golf balls I had found. However, the Women's Public Links (known as Publinx) ladies allowed me to play with them in their weekly events. The women would pick me up after I got off the school bus — before classes started — and then would drop me back off at school in time for me to catch the bus home. I played in the Detroit Area Public Links Golf Association in 1940 and 1941. If I won one of the weekly events, the prize was a U.S. Savings Bond Stamp. When I collected $18.75 worth, I was able to purchase a $25 War Bond. I also sold War Bonds in high school and won a prize for selling the most in my class.

1941. First golf photo at age 14.
Redford Golf Course, Detroit, Michigan.

The Publinx ladies were all very nice, and everybody had a good time. It was social golf with a lot of talking and laughing. However, I couldn't play in the state golf tournament unless I belonged to a private club. That's the way it was all over the nation, not just in Michigan. I knew if I wanted to play at a higher level, I would have to figure out a way to get into a private club.

When I was 16, Lakepointe Country Club gave me a membership. Finally, I got to compete against the best golfers in the area.

The country club players were a different breed. Very serious. There was hardly any talking and certainly no laughing. Every week I played at a different country club. I remember that most of the clubs were far away from my home.

When you arrived at the course, you signed in. That became the order in which you played. The first four teed off, then the next four, and so on. I played with a different group every week, and I got to know lots of women golfers. That's how I first got to play with the elite. Woo-hoo!

There was Mrs. Harley Higbie (Dorothy) who had been playing golf forever at the prestigious Country Club of Detroit. Mrs. Sam Byrd played out of Plum Hollow Golf Club. Her husband was the pro there. They weren't friendly, but they didn't scare me. I was a little red-headed kid from the other side of the tracks playing with the country club ladies. They drove up in their big Cadillacs, and I arrived in an old Dodge.

Dorothy Higbie had quite a golf pedigree. She was chosen to travel with the first American Curtis Cup Team to England in 1932. The match, which the American team won, was played at Wentworth Golf Club.

Two sisters, Harriot and Margaret Curtis, were both accomplished amateur golfers. It was their vision to create a friendly competition between the best women amateurs from the United States and England. They donated a silver bowl to be awarded to the winning team, and the competition became known as The Curtis Cup.

That first American Curtis Cup Team had an impressive roster which included: Glenna Collett Vare, Virginia Van Wie, Maureen Orcutt, Leona Cheney, Marion Hollins, and two future founding members of the LPGA, Helen Hicks and Opal Hill. Dorothy Higbie attended as a reserve but didn't play.

The Curtis Cup is still a prestigious tournament played by women amateur golfers today. The Solheim Cup is the women's professional counterpart.

Back in the early days, country clubs didn't have invitationals, guest days, and all that, like they have now. All they had were the two Detroit District Championships; one in the spring and one in the fall. The spring tournament was medal (stroke) play, and the fall event was match play. These were suspended during the war years.

In the spring of 1946, I represented Lakepointe Country Club. I won the Detroit District Medal Play Tournament and was runner-up to Mrs. Byrd in the Match Play Tournament that fall.

The following year, Lakepointe couldn't sponsor me. However, one of the Lakepointe members had a friend who belonged to Meadowbrook Country Club, and he got me in at Meadowbrook. I could only play Meadowbrook when they allowed, which turned out to be during the week, not on weekends. I represented Meadowbrook Country Club the next three years, and I believe I did them proud. I won four, and finished runner-up in one, of the six Detroit District Championships held in 1947 through 49. Not a bad showing for this young girl from the wrong side of the tracks.

I remember playing the 1948 Championship at Plum Hollow Country Club in a torrential downpour. On one of the holes, we hit our tee shot to a dry part of the fairway. We hit our second shot from there and then had to be ferried up to the elevated green in a row boat. I even parred the hole!

I always wore a visor because they were cheap — only a dollar. When it got dirty, I could throw it out and buy a new one. As soon as I could afford it, I changed from a visor to a hat for better protection from the sun. I wore hats from then on for the rest of my golf career, both playing and teaching. I also wore sunglasses because I had sunstroke when I was 12 years old.

We played for weekly prizes at the country clubs. Net and gross winners received credit certificates to be used at J.L. Hudson's Department Store, which later became Dayton-Hudson, and is now Target. I saved all that I won. At the end of the season, it was time to go back to school, so I thought I would go down to Hudson's and get something to wear. I probably had around $100, so I bought a yellow cashmere sweater. It was customary at country clubs to own a cashmere sweater. I went home, and my mother asked, "What did you get? Let me see all your new school clothes."

"All I bought is this sweater."

She said, "You can take it right back! You need a winter coat. You can't have that!"

So I took it back. I never had a cashmere sweater until years later when I told my dear friend Jane Woolley the story. She gave me

1943. Detroit City High School Golf Champion,
Redford High School, Detroit, Michigan.

one for Christmas.

In my early days, I didn't have a coach or someone to encourage me. When I got home from playing, my mother would ask, "How did you do today?"

And I would say, "Well, so-and-so beat me."

Then she would ask what I wanted for dinner, and that was the end of golf. At home, we never talked about golf or me playing the game. It was just something I did to occupy time while my mom and dad worked, and whatever I did was okay with them.

My parents didn't come to watch me much. Once, my mother came and hid behind some trees to watch me play in the state tournament. She hid because she knew I didn't want her there. It would make me nervous.

When I was in high school, Otto Hinds moved to Chemung Hills Country Club. He was the pro at Bonnie Brook who had given me the used set of irons. Chemung Hills was about 45 miles away in Howell, Michigan, which is on the Grand River. On Fridays, I would board a Greyhound bus that stopped right next to the high school, and it would take me down Grand River Avenue to Howell. Mrs. Hinds would meet me at the bus stop and drive me to the course. I would stay with them and their kids on weekends during the school year and then for the whole summer. It was a 9-hole, private country club and their living quarters were part of the clubhouse. Mr. Hinds was the golf pro and the greens keeper.

When he worked on the course, I would go out and help him. He had taken an old Model "A" car and made it into a little truck. They called it a Doodlebug. We loaded two hand-mowers in the back of the Doodlebug. He would drop me off at a green, and he would go to another one. Then he would pick me up, and we'd mow the next two greens until they were all done.

For the rough, he had a side cutter. I would ride along and lift the side-cutter bar up around the tree stumps, then put it back down. Lifting that heavy side-cutter bar was the first time I hurt my shoulder. I would whistle at him when I saw a golf ball, and he would stop so I could jump off and get the ball. I had to avoid these little snakes when I walked in the rough. I didn't like that part!

In the golf shop, we had some tables and chairs and sold beer and pop. The clubhouse itself was never open at night except for the occasional member potluck. We hosted them every so often, and I would have to stay up until everyone left, sometimes as late as 2 a.m. I would finally tell them, "Go home! We're closed now!" Then I could shut the clubhouse down and go to bed.

Next morning, I would get up early and wash clubs and clean the member's shoes. I charged a premium of 25 cents for two-tone shoes. If I caddied nine holes, I got 50 cents. So I caddied, cleaned shoes and golf clubs, tended the beer sales, and worked on the course.

Mr. Hinds let me play golf for free, but even though he was a pro, he never gave me lessons.

I used to play there with a priest who was left-handed. We played match play, and every time I got up two holes, he made me use his clubs and play left-handed until we got even. That's how I learned to play right or left-handed.

In the pro shop, we had three golf ball slot machines. They were in a case with a sliding door that could be pulled up and locked. I would watch cars that drove in. If they were people I knew, I left it open. If they were strangers, I would pull the door up and lock it since having a slot machine was illegal. We could open it up and, like any other slot machine, set it to pay after a certain number of times. When I worked in the pro shop, I would count when people played it. When it was ready to hit, I would go over with my quarter, put it in, pull the handle and win. People couldn't figure out how I won all the time!

Golf balls, at that time, were all recovered. During the war, rubber was rationed so making golf balls wasn't allowed. Golfers could turn in 12 old, cut balls to us and we would send them out to be recovered. Like tires were retreaded, golf balls were recovered. I could sell a dozen recovered balls to anyone who turned in a dozen cut balls. Then I would send the cut balls off, have them recovered, and sell them again. Everyone played with recovered golf balls.

In 1943, we moved from Bonnie Brook back into the city because my father had been rehired at the shipyard. I was starting my junior year of high school. There was gas rationing, so my father could only buy enough gas to drive to and from work. We could never go anywhere. I was no longer living in the same school district but used my friend's address so I could stay at the same school and graduate. I rode the Grand River Avenue Street car to school for two years.

During my last two years of high school, I was competing at the country clubs. There were days when I skipped school to play. At times, there would be an article the next day on the sports page of

Shirley and her parents, William and Martha Spork.

the newspaper reporting I had won. If I had a friend with me, they would take our picture, and that would be in the paper, too. Funny, I don't remember ever getting in trouble for missing classes.

On Christmas Eve my mother and I would go to Midnight Mass. We walked about a quarter of a mile to the church because my mother never drove a car. I remember walking home with her on the streets in the snow. All the Christmas tree lots were closed; everyone had gone home. A few trees were still there — free leftovers — and we picked out the tree we wanted. We carried it home through the snow and decorated it starting around two o'clock Christmas morning. That was really fun, dragging the Christmas tree down the streets of Detroit, and getting up later that morning to see our free tree all decorated. It was a special time I shared with my mother.

1945. After graduation Shirley began her college days at Michigan State Normal School, now known as Eastern Michigan University.

We lived on the ground floor of a four-unit apartment building when we moved back to the city. The family living above us had a daughter who went to Michigan State Normal School in Ypsilanti, which is now Eastern Michigan University. I didn't want to go to college. I wanted to be a professional golfer! I wanted to join the Women's Professional Golf Association (WPGA), but this girl talked my parents into sending me to college.

My mother got a loan on our furniture to pay for my tuition. The furniture of all things! You could get a loan on anything back then.

In the fall of 1945, my parents packed my bags and off I went. I didn't have a car, so I always hitched a ride. Once I rode to college in a hearse, once in a bread truck, and once in an ambulance. We would just stick our thumb out and go as far as we could. On the weekends I took my dirty clothes home, along with my books. It wasn't far, about 35 miles. Back then, Ypsilanti was just the next town out of Detroit.

I loved sports, so I majored in Physical Education (PE). It was a teaching college, so it didn't cost much to go there. I lived in the dorm, and we were on the semester system, two per year. It was somewhere around $350 for room and board which included breakfast, lunch, and dinner. Some of the kids worked in the kitchen to pay for their board.

Physical Education was a very difficult course of study because we took 25 hours per semester — 15 hours academic and then one or two additional sports classes for no credit. Students in other majors were taking just 15 hours. They didn't have to take all the extras that we did.

I had some very good PE instructors who taught me how to

teach. We were required to take classes in every sport, plus dancing which included ballroom, tap, and folk. When I started college, World War II had just ended, but rationing was still in full swing. We got a coupon for one pair of shoes per year. You just couldn't go buy shoes like you can today. I needed to have shoes for my tap dancing class, so I put taps on a pair of old shoes. I rented shoes at the bowling alley for my bowling class.

I never could figure out why I had to take classes like chemistry. I thought, "What does this have to do with being a PE teacher?" I took civics and music appreciation as electives. Household mechanics was a great class. I took it as an elective because I wanted to learn how to fix things.

During my senior year, they offered a golf class. I told the teacher I would be happy to help her since I was an experienced tournament player and knew a lot about golf.

She said, "No, you're excused from the class."

"Well thanks, I'll go practice."

I think she didn't want me around because she wasn't very good at golf. She didn't want me watching. That was fine with me. During that class time, I went over to Washtenaw Country Club. They had given me a free membership. I had an hour and a half and off I'd go. It only took five or ten minutes to get to the course which left enough time to play a few holes by myself. I didn't mind playing alone. I played with two golf balls, competing one against the other. I never got tired of practicing and playing. My mind was on golf —

not really on school.

At that time, PE students were offered the opportunity to earn a national rating to referee a sport. After I had passed the basketball rating test, I earned some spending money by refereeing at these little high schools way out in the farm towns. I had to run back and forth, back and forth on the court and got the worst leg cramps. I about died when I went to bed, but I made $15 a game. That was a lot of money for then — big stuff! I loved when I got to referee a game because then I had money to buy some snacks and gas for my car. I had finally bought my first car. It was a 1935 Dodge and cost $200. I was the only one in the dorm who had a car. Michigan has a lot of snowstorms which made getting to the games treacherous, even with my car.

These were the years when women were not supposed to excel in individual sports. Like most schools, Michigan State Normal poo-pooed it. They believed women should only play intramural sports. Well, I wanted to play in the Women's National Collegiate Golf Championship! I knew my teachers wouldn't sign my application, so one day when there was a substitute, I asked her to sign it. In 1947, my sophomore year, I paid my own way to Ohio State University to play in the National Championship. We played on the Scarlet Course, and I won! It was the only national title my college received that year. The men's athletics department honored me, but the women's wouldn't even recognize it. At the time, I didn't think about how hard it was to be a woman and play a sport, but everything I was

July, 1947. Shirley, winner of the Women's National Collegiate Golf Championship, with Grace Lenczyk, runner-up.

trying to do was twice as hard.

In 2014, Eastern Michigan University invited me to visit the campus and presented me with a varsity letter "E" for winning the Women's National Collegiate Championship in 1947. That was sixty-seven years after the fact, but better late than never. How times have changed.

Even though it was hard, there were always thoughtful people

July, 1947. Illustration from article on winning the
Women's National Collegiate Golf Championship.

who went out of their way to help. It had rained during the first day
of the tournament. My golf shoes were soaked, and I only owned
one pair. The chef in the restaurant said that he'd dry them out for
me. He stuffed them with newspaper and put them in the oven. If
it hadn't been for his generosity, I would have had to play the final
round with wet feet.

The following year, I met Marilynn Smith at the Women's

1948. Shirley met her life-long friend, Marilynn Smith, at the Women's National Collegiate Championship.

National Collegiate Championship. I was a junior, and she was a freshman at the University of Kansas. Grace Lenczyk, from Stetson University in Florida, won the tournament that year beating Marilynn in the finals.

Grace and Marilynn were matched up again in the finals the following year, and Marilynn won — capturing the 1949 National Collegiate title. After winning, Marilynn turned pro and signed a contract with Spalding. I had just graduated from college and followed a different path taking a job at Hutchins Intermediate School in Detroit.

I have gotten to know Shirley since the LPGA Founders Cup Tournament started a few years back in 2011. It has been just super to sit with her and listen to her stories about the LPGA Tour before I came along in 1977. When I hear her stories, I feel very grateful for all she did to pave the way for women not only in golf, BUT in every sport! She has helped grow the game of golf with her enthusiasm and all of her knowledge.

Thank you Shirley for all you have done in the last six decades to promote golf. Thank you for all the people you have introduced to the game and for helping them enjoy this great game as much as I have throughout the years.

You are one of the best!!

Nancy Lopez
LPGA Tour - Life Member
LPGA Teaching & Club Professional - Honorary Member
World Golf Hall of Fame

It is no exaggeration to say that Shirley Spork is a legend! She was not only one of the founders of the LPGA Tour and a fine player but went on to make her mark as one of the greatest teachers — male or female — in the history of the game.

Beyond all this, she is a delight to be around — always upbeat and positive. Shirley is an inspiration and truly a role model, not only for golfers but for anyone who wants to see how a good life is lived.

Charlie Mecham
Former LPGA Commissioner

HOLE # 2

A Teacher and a Pro

Shirley's life, up to her graduation from college, had been shaped by a burning desire to play golf, be good at it, and climb over the hurdles that were in her way. From the time she was little, Shirley had to find a way to afford to play the game she loved. There were no lessons, no junior golf, no coaching, and no fancy equipment.

The Women's Professional Golf Association (WPGA) was in operation from 1944 to 1949. Hope Seignious, Betty Hicks, and Ellen Griffin had started the WPGA Tour with the financial backing of Hope's father. He owned a cotton gin in Greensboro, North Carolina and put up the money to launch the Association and fund tournaments. Finding corporate sponsors to keep the fledgling women's Tour going after World War II was impossible, and it eventually became another post-war casualty.

While Shirley was developing her love for golf as a young girl, there were other women who shared her passion and became part of Shirley's journey near the end of her college days.

Women like Sally Sessions, Helen Hicks, and Opal Hill were

more than casual weekend golfers, as was Patty Berg, Marilynn Smith,
Louise Suggs, and others. Much has been written about Babe Didrikson
Zaharias and the incredible life she lived, and none of these pioneers
were more influential than Babe on Shirley's beginnings in golf.

Golf was all I thought about. As a seventh-grade girl, I had
looked up sports in the encyclopedia and read about the current star,
Babe Didrikson. She was a 1932 Olympic athlete who had qualified
for five events. At that time, women were only allowed to compete
in three. It was the first time the Olympic Games offered the javelin
and 80-meter hurdles events for women, and Babe won gold medals
in them both; setting a world record in the hurdles. Babe had grown
up in Beaumont, Texas, jumping hedges with the boys. That's how
she learned to jump hurdles. When she started to train, her neighbors cut their hedges the same height as the hurdles which helped her
win the gold medal.

Babe was awarded a silver medal for her high jump, even
though she tied with Jean Shiley. The judges awarded Jean the gold
medal after ruling that Babe's jump was illegal. Her technique is how
it's done today, which just goes to show that Babe was way ahead of
her time.

Babe played several sports. She even played basketball on an
Amateur Athletic Union (AAU) team. The team was sponsored by
the Employers Casualty Company who she worked for in Dallas.
She also represented them in the 1932 AAU Track and Field Cham-

pionships and single-handedly won the team title. Later she played for the House of David men's baseball team which was from my home state, Michigan. She also played pool but was not a champion. Her basketball team "Babe Didrikson's All-Americans," traveled on a vaudeville circuit and, naturally, she was paid.

Most exciting to me was that she played golf. In the early 1930s, Babe had become interested in playing golf, but she couldn't compete because there were no professional tournaments. She won the first tournament she entered, the 1935 Texas State Invitational. After that, the United States Golf Association (USGA) took away her amateur status. Back then, if you made money in another sport or worked in the golf business, like Helen Hicks, you couldn't compete in amateur tournaments. So she was deemed to be a professional whether she wanted to be or not.

Babe dominated women's golf with drives of 250 yards, along with great putts. I also read about Patty Berg and how women golfers were playing in the U.S. Women's Amateur, the Women's Western Open, and the Women's Trans-Mississippi Championship.

There weren't many professional tournaments at the time, so Babe fought to get her amateur status back. She was finally reinstated as an amateur in 1943. Babe won the 1946 U.S. Women's Amateur Golf Championship at Southern Hills Country Club in Tulsa, Oklahoma. The following year, she was the first American to win the Women's British Amateur. After she returned to the U.S., she wasn't happy as an amateur. Babe wanted to excel and make money, so she turned pro. There was little money in women's professional golf, but you were allowed to make absolutely no money in amateur golf.

In January 1949, Babe and Patty Berg went to Wilson Sporting Goods President, L.B. Icely, and told him they needed a tour so they could compete. By then the WPGA was all but over. The idea interested Icely, so Wilson put up some money and hired Fred Corcoran to be the tournament director for three years. After the first year, Spalding and MacGregor joined with Wilson to pay Fred's salary. Fred had been the men's PGA Tour manager and also managed baseball players like Ted Williams and Stan Musial. He was also Babe Didrikson's manager.

Fred had his lawyer draw up the charter for the new tour which he named the Ladies Professional Golf Association (LPGA) in 1949. His lawyer's office was in New York, and the law required that someone living in the state of New York had to sign it. They contacted Helen Hicks who lived on Long Island, and she agreed to sign the charter.

Patty Berg, Helen Dettweiler, Sally Sessions, and Betty Jameson, were playing in The Eastern Championship at Essex Falls Country Club in New Jersey in May 1949. While there, Fred got them to sign the charter. They elected Patty to be the first president. Helen was vice president, Sally was secretary, and Betty was treasurer.

Before the LPGA, the WPGA sanctioned tournaments. The Titleholders Championship was played at Augusta Country Club, which backs up to Augusta National Golf Club (where they hold the

Masters). The Titleholders was by invitation only, both for amateurs and professionals. As the reigning National Collegiate Champion, I was invited to compete and was so excited to play with these top professionals. The tournament was in March 1948, and Patty won.

After the tournament, Patty asked if I would like to drive her car back to Chicago. "I don't need it now," she said. "Take it to the parking garage and then call the number on this piece of paper. Wilson Sporting Goods will send a man over for the keys. Then you can take the train or bus back to Detroit which should save you some money."

Wow, that was really something! I was going to drive Patty Berg's car, and she had just won the Titleholders! She met me at the car on Monday morning. Her clubs were boxed up and locked in the trunk, so I put my stuff in the back seat. I took off, drove all day, and stopped for the night at a motel.

The next morning I was driving through Kentucky and on the radio, I hear about Patty Berg winning the Titleholders. "Yes, and I'm driving her car! I've got her clubs in the trunk!"

I was near Paducah, Kentucky and the guy following me started tooting his horn. He was pointing at my car and gesturing. I thought I must have a flat tire, so I pulled to the side of the road. I got out and checked, but they looked fine to me. I walk around the back again, and then I saw it — the trunk was cracked open about four inches. I pulled the lid up, and there were no golf clubs inside. No golf clubs! Now, what do I do?

I drove back over 100 miles looking for the clubs in the ditch. I stopped at the gas station where I had filled up that morning and asked the attendant if he remembered seeing my trunk open. He couldn't remember, so I drove to the police station. Once there, I explained who I was and told them that in the last 24 hours I had lost some golf clubs . . . Patty Berg's golf clubs!

They made out a report and off I went to Chicago thinking, "What in the world am I going to tell the person picking up Patty's car?" I got to Chicago and met up with the man from Wilson Sporting Goods. I said, "I have some bad news. I've lost Patty's clubs."

He replied, "Oh don't worry about it! She gets new clubs every two or three months. She won't mind."

"Well," I thought, "how am I going to tell Patty? I'm not going to see her for a while, so I need to call and tell her." Her reaction was the same, "Don't worry about it!"

Every time I saw her after that, we always had a standing joke — do you have some clubs you'd like to lose? If so, just let me know! Patty and I were very good friends through the years. We shared a lot of time together, even used to attend Mass together on Sundays.

That summer Betty Hicks was in Detroit to promote the third U.S. Women's Open Golf Championship at the Atlantic City Country Club in Northfield, New Jersey. It was in August 1948, and Betty was going to drive to the tournament. She said to me, "You sign up, and I'll pay for your room in the hotel. You can also ride with me." I didn't have any money, so if it hadn't been for her, I would not have been able to play. She was a friend, helping me during that phase of my career. Betty played a great tournament, finishing runner-up to Babe.

Marilynn, who I had just met at the National Collegiate Championship, was also playing and we were paired. We were playing terribly, so we started singing. This other player in our group got really upset with us. She went to the committee after the ninth hole and told them we were bothering her game. It reminded me of the days when I first played with the serious country club ladies, and as we walked to the 10th tee, I whispered to Marilynn, "Don't you even say a word to her!" So we didn't say BOO for the next couple of hours. After we finished the back nine, this gal walked over to us and complained, "You didn't say anything to me!"

"Well, we didn't want to be responsible for ruining your game," I answered. Marilynn just smiled, and we walked away. That was the end of that.

Women's golf was developing, but professional numbers were growing slowly. Babe was adamant she wanted more competition. The day I turned pro was May 6, 1950, at Skycrest Country Club in Chicago where Babe was the new head pro. I had just graduated college and was teaching in the Detroit public schools. I was eating breakfast with Marilynn, Babe, and Babe's husband, George Zaharias, the morning of the opening round of the Chicago Weathervane.

Babe says to me, "Listen, kid, why don't you turn pro?"

I said, "Well yeah, I'd like to turn pro."

"We need numbers! We need people!"

"Well, how do I become a pro?"

Babe stood up, walked around the table, smacked me on top of the head and said, "I pronounce you a pro! Now go down to the first tee and tell them you're a pro."

Now, it's quite a walk down the hill to the first tee and all the way down I was thinking, "Should I? Shouldn't I? Should I? Shouldn't I?"

When I finally arrived at the first tee, I said, "Excuse me, Mrs. Dennehy. Please announce me as a pro."

Mrs. Dennehy's jaw dropped. "Does your mother know this?"

"No, but she will tonight when I call and tell her."

Of course, this was big news back home. It was a few days before my 23rd birthday. I was from Michigan State Normal, had won the National Collegiate Championship, and was reigning Michigan State Amateur Champion. I was leaving the amateur world behind me and turning pro. Big stuff!

The temperature was in the low 40s, and the wind was blowing 50 miles an hour. When I set my ball on the tee, the wind blew it off. On one hole, my ball was in the rough. The wind caught me in the middle of my backswing. I lost my balance and totally missed the ball. Whiffed it! I was playing with Marilynn, and we just laughed.

Par on Skycrest was 74, and Louise Suggs shot an unbelievable 76 in the wind! This was my first round as a pro, and I shot a 95. Marilynn shot a 93. It was a rough day.

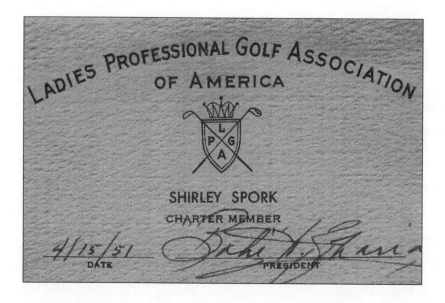

1951. Shirley's first membership card, signed by Babe Zaharias.

In October 1950, I was going to teach and coach at Bowling Green State University while studying for my master's degree. I had signed a contract to start in the fall. The U.S. Women's Open was at Rolling Hills Country Club in Wichita, Kansas, in September. Since it was before school started, I was able to play.

We were winding up our first full year of the LPGA Tour, and after the final round of the Open, an organizational meeting was called. Eight more of us signed the charter: Alice and Marlene Bauer, Bettye Danoff, Marilynn Smith, Opal Hill, Louise Suggs, Babe, and me. That is how we became the 13 founding members of the LPGA. That's how it started.

During the early 1950s, we were just out there at the mercy of anyone who would put up some money. It was the job of our tournament director, Fred Corcoran, to find sponsors to fund the Tour and make all the arrangements. Back then the big three attractions were Patty, Louise, and the Babe. Next came Marilynn and a few other top players.

When the next Tour season started in January 1951, I was teaching Monday through Thursday at Bowling Green. The first three tournaments that year were in Florida. As soon as I finished classes on Thursday, I would drive 75 miles to the Willow Run Airport (just outside of Ypsilanti, Michigan) get on a plane and fly to the Tour stop. I could play Friday, Saturday, and Sunday, then go back and teach. That's how I played the Tour at the beginning of my career. I would rush to the airport after teaching, fly to the Tour stop, and then tee it up without playing a practice round or seeing the golf course. Marilynn made notes of the clubs she used on each hole during her practice rounds and shared them with me. When I got to a hole, I'd look at her notes and think, "Well Marilynn hit a four iron here, so it must be a four iron." I was playing blind.

I was a teacher and a player. I had graduated with a teaching degree from college and was surprised that none of the players on the LPGA Tour really knew anything about their swings. I asked Louise if I could take a movie picture of her swing to show my students. "Well," she said, "I don't want to see it!" None of them wanted to see their swings. How very different from the Tour players of today.

I did learn a lot from sitting and watching Marilynn take lessons when we traveled together. I would listen to what the pro was telling her and then I would try it myself.

At that time, three major PGA Pros taught women: Tommy Armour, Jerry Glynn, and Harry Pressler. Harry was far away in California, so more often the ladies went to Jerry or Tommy if they wanted a lesson. Patty took lessons from Les Bolstad who was a prominent teacher and longtime coach at the University of Minnesota. Patty worked with Les her entire career.

In general, nobody wanted help because they wanted to do it themselves. Some of us, except for Louise and Babe, talked about our swings.

In those early days of the LPGA Tour, I would teach for nine months and play in the summer. I did get to play in a few tournaments during the school year (if they were close), but I didn't have the money to be out on the Tour full-time.

Other players were sponsored: Patty and Babe by Wilson, Marilynn by Spalding, and Louise by MacGregor. These equipment companies paid their tournament fees and expenses. They also paid royalties for selling the player's line of golf clubs and for the pro giving clinics and playing exhibitions.

Golfcraft was the fourth largest manufacturer of golf equipment but was not sponsoring anyone on the LPGA Tour. I wrote a letter to the owner, Mr. Ted Woolley. I told him that I was teaching at Bowling Green State University and he needed a woman to give clinics because that is what his competitors were doing. He invited

1950. Ted Woolley (owner of Golfcraft), Shirley, and Fred Haas, Sr. (general manager). Shirley signing her contract to join the Golfcraft professional staff.

me to their office in Chicago. After we talked, I signed a contract. I quit my job at Bowling Green to concentrate on playing, now that I had a sponsor.

Golfcraft made a set of clubs with my name on them. These were called signature clubs. They arranged exhibitions for me to play and promote their company. I got a monthly royalty check for every club of mine that they sold. They paid me seven cents per club. They also paid my expenses. That's how I had an income.

Mr. Woolley had bought a golf company that had an inventory of metal shafts. You couldn't make clubs during the war because of the steel. After the war ended, Mr. Woolley started the Golfcraft Company. He was able to start making clubs immediately and compete with the three main club companies because he had golf shafts in stock. Metal suppliers weren't going to sell to the new guy; they were going to service Wilson, Spalding, and MacGregor. So Mr. Woolley was able to get the jump on them because he had the shafts. That's how he got ahead.

Mr. Woolley bought a machine that drilled holes. It was a surplus from the war, and I believe it was called a Kingman machine. During the war, it was used to manufacture torpedoes. It was round with several spokes and was used to drill the hosel so the shaft could be connected to the club head. The club head rotated on the machine, and each spoke reamed the hole in the hosel a little larger. It had to be done gradually, or you'd crack the head. Once the hosel was reamed out, they attached the club head to the shaft and pinned it. All iron clubs were pinned.

For the woods, they bought blocks of persimmon from Tennessee and used milling machines to round and buff them off. All the companies made persimmon heads. The heads that had flaws in them were painted black so the knot couldn't be seen. These were sold as store clubs and were less expensive. The clubs that were pure grained and flawless would be stained with various finishes like walnut and cherry and were sold for quite a bit more money.

We had two types of accounts (pro shops at golf facilities and the sporting goods stores) and made a line of clubs for each. The real money was made off the sporting goods store line. Each store would order 50 sets while the pro shops only ordered five sets. The pro shop clubs, which Golfcraft called "Pro Zone," were the most expensive, so the sporting goods line outsold them 10 to one.

What the manufacturers did was set up a storage area in their factory. They made equipment and put it in a bin with a fence around it. That was called a Government Warehouse. Because it was bonded, you had proof that the merchandise had been made and then billed whoever had ordered the equipment, like Sears & Roebuck. Golf companies would manufacture and stockpile equipment during the slow months to be ready to ship to their customers at a later date. This is how they paid their workers in the off season and how businesses could function year-round. Come spring; the customer (like Sears & Roebuck) would buy the goods back from themselves to avoid a tax. All companies did that, including Golfcraft.

I worked for Golfcraft and traveled between tournaments giving clinics. I would visit a golf course where one of the pros was on the Golfcraft staff. Many times I traveled with Marilynn who represented Spalding. The club would advertise that we were coming on a certain date and time. For the first hour or so we would greet people, followed by an exhibition demonstrating the right way and the wrong way to hit a golf ball. We entertained them by doing funny little things like trick shots. I had clubs that I could hit right-handed and ones I could hit left-handed. I could bend the shaft on one to show how to hit around a tree. I made the clinic entertaining, as well as instructive.

It was at Golfcraft that I met a lifelong friend, Jane Woolley. She had gone to St. Mary's College and then on to the University of Notre Dame. When Jane attended St. Mary's College, students weren't allowed to take classes at the University of Notre Dame, but that has since changed. Jane also studied at the Chicago Art Institute and became a successful artist and advertising agent.

Jane was Mr. Woolley's daughter and handled the advertising for her father's company. She was also responsible for managing the Golfcraft advisory staff. Besides myself, she managed Lloyd Mangrum, Fred Haas Jr., Joe Kirkwood Jr., Ralph Guldahl, and two or three other men. She kept track of royalties for all the signature clubs sold and made our travel schedules.

Before I signed with them, the only set of lady clubs Golfcraft manufactured was named for Jane — Jane Carol. I still have an entire set of them.

One weekend, Mr. Woolley had gone to watch the Masters Golf Tournament in Augusta, Georgia. While he was gone, a union rep came to the factory and talked the employees into joining. Mr. Woolley came back and was told the shop was going to unionize. "No," he said, "you aren't going to do that in my shop." To get around unionization, Mr. Woolley packed up his company and moved it to Escondido, near San Diego, California. This was in 1952. He told his employees that the company would cover the expenses for anyone wanting to move to the West Coast. The Woolley family (which was just Jane and her parents) moved, along with all the key people. Mr. Woolley built a new factory and started over on the West Coast.

The Woolley's sold their house in Oak Park, Illinois. They bought a beautiful two-story Spanish hacienda, sitting on several acres, in Rancho Santa Fe, and lived in a small motel room for months until all the renovations were finished. The house hadn't been lived in during the war and needed a lot of work. The pool was totally full of eucalyptus branches and leaves. They didn't even know they had a pool until the gardeners started cleaning up the grounds and found it! They planted citrus trees all over the property. Everything was stunning when the renovations were completed, and I remember this great big porch that encircled the entire house.

To live in the Covenant development in Rancho Santa Fe, you had to own at least five acres. That gave you a golf membership at the private Rancho Santa Fe Golf Club.

Jane later moved to Los Angeles. She worked for B.D. Howes and Son, a fine jeweler on Wilshire Boulevard across from Bullocks. They had stores in Pasadena, Santa Barbara, Newport Beach, and Los Angeles. She sketched pictures of diamonds and learned how to illustrate on a scratch board. Jane also continued to do all the Golfcraft advertising and produced their catalogs, taking all the pictures herself.

After Jane moved to Los Angeles, she played golf at Rancho Park Golf Course. I had a house in the Palm Springs area. Jane would

Golfcraft's "Big Three" - Shirley Englehorn (Little Shirley),
Jane Woolley, Shirley Spork.

come on the train to visit, and I would drive to the north side of
town to pick her up.

Indian Wells Country Club opened in 1955. Jane would
spend the weekend with me and play golf there while I was teaching
at Tamarisk Country Club. Before long, she bought a condo at Indian Wells and was one of their first members.

Jane was quite a golfer and could outdrive me. She was the
club champion at Indian Wells for 10 straight years from 1968 to
1977. She and Beverly Hallmeyer started the Ten and Under (TAU)
Club for women in Southern California. To be a member, you had

to have a handicap of 10 or less, and they played at various courses. I sponsored a Shirley Spork Cup which was given to the winner each year.

I've lived in the Palm Springs area for most of the last seven decades, and it's been amazing to see the changes. When I first moved here, there were four golf courses; two 18-hole and two 9-hole. Now there are over 120 courses. Who would have ever thought there'd be so many golf courses built in the middle of the desert?

1951. Penfold announcing Shirley's European exhibition tour.

I have known Shirley since I was a teenager and I always look forward to seeing her! She has a wonderful, positive, upbeat attitude. She also, in fact, has an enduring knowledge of our game. From the game itself, to the history of the LPGA, and the women's game, she has lived it. Shirley has been one of the premier teachers for many years.

I have watched her take great pleasure in the achievements of today's wonderful players. The LPGA has rightfully celebrated her role as a "founder." Thank you, Shirley!

Judy Rankin

LPGA Tour - Life Member

LPGA Teaching & Club Professional - Honorary Member

World Golf Hall of Fame

Shirley was a founder of the LPGA. Without her love and passion for the game and the LPGA Tour, there would be no place for women to play and have a wonderful career. She was a role model for all future pros and she set the highest standards to teach the fundamentals of the game. She is a national treasure in the women's game of golf.

Thank you — it was an honor to have played with you.

Pat Bradley

LPGA Tour - Life Member

World Golf Hall of Fame

HOLE # 3

Early Days of the Tour

What might, on the outside, seem like a glamorous life, was any-thing but. This group of young women wore countless hats. They served as chauffeurs, chefs, publicists, coaches, trainers, rules officials, and much, much more. They ran their own show and had great fun doing it. These women crisscrossed the country trying to eke out a living playing profes-sional golf.

In the early days of the LPGA Tour, we took care of most things ourselves. Each of us had a job. Some of us were on the rules committee, some marked the course, some were in charge of the clinic, and so on. We set up the courses ourselves and were our own rules officials during the tournaments. Our tournament director, Fred Corcoran, hired an ex-caddy named Spec Hammond. Spec followed us around the country with a card table and a bullhorn that he used to announce us on the tee.

We hosted a cocktail party, usually on the Wednesday or Thursday night before the tournament and paid for it ourselves. We invited the local press to come to the party so they would know who we were and help us get the word out.

The cocktail parties were just one part of our promotion duties. We gave live interviews at the local radio stations, and Fred gave us posters to put up anywhere and everywhere we could. We would go to the gas station, the drug store, and the grocery store and ask them to put our sign in their window. We spoke to local civic groups, such as the Lions or Rotary Club. We did whatever we could to get local participation. Come to the golf course; the LPGA is in town!

At every tournament, we gave a clinic called the "Swing Parade." We each hit different shots and Patty Berg was usually the mistress of ceremonies. I gave a trick-shot clinic, dressed as a clown, and did all kinds of goofy things. We had a lot of fun.

We were in Baltimore, and I was giving my trick-shot clinic. Charles Boswell was there. "Charlie" had played football and baseball for the University of Alabama. He was blinded in the Battle of the Bulge but went on to win the National Blind Golf Championship title 17 times in addition to 11 international championships for blind golfers. He was quite a player. In 1958, he was the recipient of the Ben Hogan Trophy given by the Golf Writers Association of America. After the clinic, at the cocktail party, he came up to me and said, "I really enjoyed you hitting the 'tree club' which was that bent club you used. I also enjoyed your two-sided club."

I asked, "How did you know I used those clubs?"

He replied, "From what you said, I could picture what you

were doing."

When we played in a small town that had a baseball farm team we would talk to the manager. If a game was scheduled while we were there, often they would allow us to go out on the field and hit shots to entertain the crowd before the game started. We could only hit wedges or short irons because the fields were only about 350 feet. Sometimes Babe Zaharias would hit tennis balls into the crowd which was dangerous. Fred didn't allow that very long, so Babe hit golf balls over the outfield wall.

One time we were playing a tournament in St. Louis. Marilynn Smith is a big Cardinals fan, so we (along with Babe and her husband George) went to the game. While we were watching the game, Babe was eating popcorn. She'd toss it up into the air and catch it in her mouth. She never missed! Next thing you know, Marilynn and I were trying our luck. There was popcorn all over the bleachers, but not one piece in our mouths. Finally, Marilynn and I each caught one, and I started to try it again. Babe grabbed my arm and said, "Listen, kid, once you do it, don't do it again." I've never forgotten that statement; *once you've done it, don't do it again.*

We also learned the history of the towns where we played. We would visit historical monuments, museums, or anything unique to that part of the country. I can even remember visiting the Baseball Hall of Fame in Cooperstown, New York.

On Sunday nights before we left town, we would find a pay phone and call the Associated Press, United Press International, and

Golf World. It was up to us to call in the results if we wanted any coverage. We would tell them where the next stop was, hoping to get some pre-publicity. *Golf World* was the only publication that consistently printed results of our tournaments. After we had made our calls, we would drive until dark.

The Holiday Inn hotel chain was just beginning in the 1950s. When we could find one, we'd stay there. The nice thing about the Holiday Inn was that you could book ahead for the next tournament location and you were guaranteed a room. Remember, this was before you could hold a room with a credit card. So, it was Holiday Inn — drive, Holiday Inn — drive, Holiday Inn — drive. That was how we got across the country. Sometimes we stayed in a country club member's home which was an extra special treat.

We drove in caravans and used ping pong paddles to communicate between cars by sticking them out the car window. We didn't have CB radios or cell phones. We used green, red, and yellow paddles . . . green to eat, red for gas, and yellow for a potty stop. If we saw a cop, we'd tap our brake lights to warn the rest of the caravan. Fortunately, we never had any serious accidents.

This was before interstate highways were built, so we traveled through a lot of small towns. I rode with Marilynn my first year. Spalding had given her a car, and I got to ride along for free. We would stop in some of the cutest, quaint towns. She had two baseball gloves which she had negotiated as part of her Spalding contract. We would drive for an hour or two, hop out of the car, run around

1950s. Shirley modeling the tire kit for the Ford Thunderbird.

the town park, play catch, get back in the car, and drive some more. That's how we got our exercise. Sometimes we would drive 500 miles or even 800 miles between tournaments. We spent a lot of time on the road.

During our miles and miles on the road, we got tired of eating at diners. Sometimes our only vegetable was a wedge of lettuce, canned peas, or carrots. We looked for cafeterias, places where we could get some fresh vegetables. We also tried to find a motel that had a kitchenette so we could cook. When we found one, we would stop at a grocery store and buy the ingredients we needed to prepare our meals. One of the girls had a frying pan, someone else lugged around a coffee pot, and I had a shoebox of spices. We could cook spaghetti or some other meal. We ate a lot of canned tuna and liver because the iron was good for our strength. Marilynn had some kind of vitamins that she thought everyone should take. We tried to eat a healthy diet. We didn't have a nutritionist. We didn't have a trainer. We didn't have a manager. We just helped each other out and did the best we could.

Today's players have a fitness van that follows them from Tour stop to Tour stop. We trained by hitting balls. We were very accurate. Very seldom did we ever, ever, hit a ball out of bounds. We didn't worry about distance, all we worried about was hitting the ball straight. We were target oriented, and we liked to practice. We hit lots of golf balls and never thought of hitting further than the next person since we all hit our drives about 225 yards. The exception was Babe. She was the long hitter of the early LPGA Tour. When Mickey Wright joined the Tour in 1955, she became our long hitter.

The purses we played for weren't very big. Many of them were around $3,000. I remember playing in Waterloo, Iowa in 1958. It was the Waterloo Open at Sunnyside Golf Course, and I played with the Monsignor from the local Catholic Church in the pro-am. Sunday morning I went to Mass before teeing off and put a check in the collection plate. A couple weeks later I got a letter from the Monsignor and my check back. He said, "I enjoyed playing in the pro-am with you. You didn't do so well in the tournament, and I think you need this more than the church does." He invited me to stay at the rectory for free the next time I was going through Waterloo. He added, "I have a wonderful housekeeper who will take good care of you. Drop in any time. I'm also sending you the ladies cookbook that we're selling."

Anytime I flew into Chicago, I went to church at the small airport chapel in the basement. They had one in Boston, too. I received a letter from an airport priest also. The note said, "I see you flew through again. Thanks for your check. I hope you are doing well in your golf."

In the early 1950's, new golf courses were springing up throughout the country. They wanted a Tour event to put them on the map. Because the courses were so rough, the men's PGA Tour wouldn't play them, but we did.

I remember playing on a new course on the east side of Albuquerque, New Mexico. It was called Four Hills Country Club. Rattlesnakes were everywhere! You could see them on the driving range. There were mounds in the fairways, and the snakes seemed to gather at the bottom of each mound looking for some shade. The snakes were all over the place, and we were careful to stay away from them. When we'd come off the course, instead of asking, "How did you play," we would ask each other, "how many snakes did you see today?"

Once we were playing in Ardmore, Oklahoma. Opie Turner hosted a tournament at Dornick Hills Country Club. Her husband, Waco, was a multi-millionaire oil man and they both loved golf. The couple knew that most of us pros were struggling financially, so they paid extra money for birdies, eagles, and the low round of the day. Heck, they even gave away money if they saw you hit a great shot. Opie and Waco walked around the course and watched us play. Each carried a sack of money, and it seemed like they couldn't wait to hand some out. It was one of the strangest things I ever saw while competing on the Tour. Marilynn came inches away from a hole-in-one. That would have paid $1,000. BIG money in 1954!

Babe and Betty Dodd played in that tournament. When Babe arrived, she said, "I'm going to win this tournament. When they present the prizes, I want a Palomino horse. I'll get up on that horse and ride it off the course."

"Babe, what are you going to do with this horse afterwards?" Betty asked.

"Aw, I don't know. It would just be a fun thing to do."

Patty won the tournament, but Opie gave Babe a horse anyway. And just like she said, Babe got on it and rode off down the fairway.

Later Betty asked, "Babe what did you do with that horse?"

"I rode it a couple of miles down the road. Then I gave it back to Opie."

It was the damndest thing.

A few years later, Waco had a falling out with the board members at Dornick Hills Country Club, so he decided to build his own golf course. He named it after himself, the Waco Turner Golf Course.

1950s. Betty Dodd, Betty Bush, Shirley.

We played there soon after it opened and were allowed to pick weeds on the greens before we hit our putts. We also had to play the same cup position all week because the greens were so hard. Two of our player's husbands dug a cup in each green using a trowel, and that's where the pin remained for all three rounds. Regardless of the conditions we just played anywhere!

Once when we played in the Wendell-West Golf Tournament in Oceans Shore, Washington, military reserve airplanes were using one of the golf holes as an airstrip. They were on a search and rescue mission of a plane that had gone down in the Pacific Ocean. We had to wait for a signal from a tournament official to know when we could play that hole.

Then there was the Mickey Wright Invitational at La Jolla Country Club which is in San Diego County in Southern California. It's right near the coast, and there was an awful heat wave. We played on the hottest day ever recorded in San Diego. It was 111 degrees! They canceled Friday's round due to the heat and smog. We played Saturday and Sunday in the stifling heat. There wasn't any air conditioning at the motels or restaurants. We pulled the mattresses off our beds and put them out on the balcony to try and sleep. It was miserable! I couldn't wait to get back to Palm Desert. At least in the desert, we had good air conditioning!

We played numerous events throughout Texas during the tornado season. We were always on alert for the siren to sound stopping play. When it did, we'd mark our ball and head to the nearest shelter.

If there was a lightning storm and we couldn't get to a shelter, we'd find the deepest sand bunker, take our spikes off and sit up against the wall.

One time we saw a funnel cloud forming in the distance and felt the wind picking up. I was in the middle of the fairway contemplating what club to use to carry over a stream to the par-five green. The wind was at my back, and I kept changing clubs. By the time I hit the shot, I'd gone from a fairway wood to a short iron, and the wind carried my ball onto the green. Then the siren sounded, and we hurried to the shelter.

I once drove a 385-yard, par-four hole. A gust of wind came up, caught my ball and carried it onto the green while the group

April, 1952. Betty Dodd, Peggy Kirk Bell, Shirley, Betty Bush and Patty Berg fly to Corpus Christi, Texas for a one-day tournament on the Saturday of Easter Weekend.

ahead was putting. That shocked all of us. My longest drive ever!

In the early 1960s, we were playing Pecan Valley Golf Club in San Antonio, Texas. An earthen dike broke upstream, miles from the golf course, sending a flash flood cutting across one of the fairways. Once we hit our approach shot over the raging water and onto the green, we'd jump into a waiting jeep. The driver would gun the engine to get a running start. We got soaked as the jeep slid through the river, but it was the only way to get to the green and finish our round. There never seemed to be a dull moment on the LPGA Tour!

In the early days, most of us traveled by car. One of our first flights as a group was on a DC-3. We had just finished the two-day Houston Weathervane Tournament and were heading to Corpus Christi. Babe knew people all around the country, especially in Texas. She would get someone to put up money for a one-day event and whoever was available would show up and play. It gave us a chance to make a little extra money and introduced more people to the women's Tour. At this event, the boys had never caddied before. They didn't know how to carry a golf bag, and some didn't speak English. So, in addition to playing, we were teaching them how to caddy. Quite a difference from today's Tour.

I remember once playing in a tournament in Florida, and my score was lower than Babe's that day. When she came in, she said, "What'd you shoot today, kid?"

I said, "73."

"You beat me. How'd you do that?"

"I guess I played better than you did." Nobody ever talked to Babe like that!

"I guess you're right, kid," she said with a laugh.

At one tournament I was working on my pitch shots. Babe was really good at them. She came up to me and said, "You want to know how to do that? Watch this." She took my club, hit the shot, and walked away. She didn't explain how to do it; she just hit it and left.

Babe was a great entertainer, and she had quite an attitude.

She never doubted her own abilities, and because of that, she offended some people. She would walk up to us and say, "Well, The Babe is here! Who's going to be second?" She had tremendous self-confidence!

Babe also played the harmonica and sang. Betty Dodd played the guitar and performed with Babe when we would entertain guests during some of our Tour stops. Babe performed on the *Ed Sullivan Show* in 1953 and recorded songs on the Mercury Records label that were sold in stores. Her biggest seller was a record with "I Felt a Little Teardrop" on one side and "Detour" on the other.

Babe also loved to play gin rummy. When she arrived at a country club, she'd ask, "Who's the best gin player? I'll play 'em!"

Babe liked to dress well and always had her nails and hair done beautifully. She had help with her appearance from her good friend, Bertha Bowen, who was a wealthy woman from Fort Worth, Texas.

In 1951, Babe and George bought Forest Hills Golf and Country Club in Tampa, Florida. A couple years later, Babe was diagnosed with colon cancer. She was only 45 when she died in 1956 but accomplished a great deal in her short life. She was **the** drawing card of the early LPGA Tour.

These were hard times by today's standards, not that playing the Tour today is an easy life. We had nothing to compare our experiences with since we were blazing a new trail. Our personalities made the Tour, and the Tour made us.

1950s. Shirley leaving New Mexico after a tournament.

April, 1952. Shirley's caddie, golf professional J.D. Taylor and Shirley at a tournament in Clovis, New Mexico. Notice the large gallery.

There are wonderful stories to be told about the beginning days of the LPGA and no one can tell them better and more accurately than Shirley Spork. Shirley is one of the 13 original LPGA founding members, former Tour player, an incredible teacher for over sixty years, and one of the country's longtime promoters of women's golf.

Shirley shares in this book her great insights into the struggles and successes of professional women's golf in the early years and the growth in the years which followed. If you love golf, you will love the tales in this book.

Dr. Gary Wiren

PGA - Master Professional

PGA Hall of Fame

World Golf Teachers Hall of Fame

I have known Shirley for over 60 years. We first met when I was her student and we soon became friends. I am now 90 years old and still play 18 holes. When my golf swing disappears, I can always find it by remembering Shirley's teaching.

Thank you, Shirley, for my golf swing and your friendship.

Helen Knight

Student and Friend

39-time Women's Club Champion,

El Caballero Country Club, Tarzana, California

HOLE # 4

At a Crossroad

Shirley had graduated from college with a teaching degree in physical education. A few months later she would leave the amateur world behind her becoming a pro in the sport she loved. So, what next? Play or teach? Take the ultimate gamble of "life on the road" or find a place to hang out a shingle and help others with their golf games. Sometimes you plan your path. Sometimes it merely unfolds before you day by day.

I met Joey Rey in 1951. He said, "You're not going to make it on the Tour, you should get a club job."

Joey was raised in Los Angeles near Dodger Stadium. He played alto sax in a band and met his wife Ginger playing a gig in Clearlake, a town about 100 miles northwest of Sacramento.

Joey worked for Rosenberg Brothers, a dried fruit packing company in the San Joaquin and Sacramento Valleys. He traveled around to all the farms and bought their fruits and nuts. Joey contracted a lung disease from the fumigants and because of that had

1968. Joey Rey and Shirley. Joey was Shirley's mentor.

to live where it was moist. When he would come to the desert, he couldn't breathe well.

Joey was a good amateur golfer and in 1948 became the head golf professional at the prestigious Pasatiempo Golf Club in Santa Cruz, California.

Pasatiempo has quite a history. It was one of three golf courses developed by the great woman amateur golfer, Marion Hollins, and was designed by the legendary Scottish architect, Alister MacKenzie. Pasatiempo opened in 1929 and was the playground of the rich and famous. The following year, Marion brought in the legendary Ernest Jones to be the resident teaching pro. Ernest taught several of the leading women amateur golfers of the day including Virginia Van Wie, Glenna Collett Vare, and Betty Hicks who later became a professional.

Joey said, "Why don't you come here and give lessons when you're not playing in tournaments?" So I did. I finished my year at Bowling Green State University where I was teaching and headed to Santa Cruz in July of 1952. That was the first teaching job I had at a semi-private club.

Joey started one of the first junior golf programs in Northern California. It was called Monterey Bay Area Junior Golf Association. Southern California already had a well-established junior program, and Joey helped develop a tournament between the two.

Joey gave all his time to other people. He never had a lot materially because he gave it all away . . . he helped everybody! Joey really influenced me, at the beginning of my career, to be more giving and interested in others.

People in the military stationed at Fort Ord played at Pasatiempo because they didn't have a golf course on base. Even the commanding officer came to us for lessons. Joey finally asked him, "Why do you come over here when I could come to the base? You have a lot of room. Mow a field off, and we'll put in a driving range. Later we can talk about building a golf course." So that's how the golf course got started at Fort Ord.

Military personnel were allowed to be members of Monterey Peninsula Country Club in Pebble Beach at a rate cheaper than cheap. They didn't buy anything there because they could buy all their equipment from the Post Exchange (PX). We kidded them that if it were possible, they would have even re-shafted their tees!

Joey had heard about the death of a golf pro in Ukiah, which was about 190 miles north of Pasatiempo Golf Club. This was late in 1952. He suggested I go up there, give a clinic, and apply for the job. He said that if I got the job, I could play tournaments in the winter when it was raining in Ukiah. The city council hired me and allowed me to play the winter circuit before starting my new job on March 1, 1953. It was here, at this little 9-hole municipal golf course, that I worked as a head pro for the first time in my career.

I worked there all year and became good friends with several of the locals. I was dating Bob Rogers. His parents were caretakers of a large piece of property near Willets, which was about 20 miles or so from Ukiah.

At Christmastime, we borrowed a pickup truck from my friend, Joe Weber, who owned the Buick dealership in Ukiah. Joe's daughter, Patty, and a friend, Timmy, went with Bob and me up to Willets to cut down a Christmas tree for my pro shop. Soon after we arrived, we found the perfect tree, cut it down, and put it in the bed of the pickup. Then we saw another one we liked. We cut it down and loaded it. There was another one we thought someone else might like. We kept going and soon we had a pickup truck full of Christmas trees!

We took them back to my yard, which was just a short walk

*1953. Shirley awarding trophies at her first
Junior Boy's Tournament, Ukiah, California.*

from the clubhouse, and set them all up. When the golfers, who I had come to know throughout the year, came into the pro shop, I asked them if they had bought a tree. If they said no, I'd tell them, "Go over to my place and pick one out." That was my first Christmas tree lot, and I was so excited to share the trees, which I had chopped down, with my new friends. It reminded me of my childhood when my mother and I would pick out our free Christmas tree after Midnight Mass and drag it home through the streets of Detroit.

The tree I put up in my golf shop was decorated with head covers. I also strung tees in a garland fashion and attached little hooks on golf balls for ornaments. It looked great and was such fun.

While I was working at Ukiah, I applied to be the golf coach at Stanford University in Palo Alto, California and got the job. They were going to let me finish my master's degree — tuition free — and pay me $3,800 for the season. I told them I couldn't live on that. I said maybe I could make ends meet with the royalties I earned from my signature golf clubs. They objected to that. I explained to them it was no different than a professor making royalties off a book, but they didn't budge. Next, I suggested I could go down to the local golf course and give lessons at night, so I could earn enough money to live on. They were opposed to that too!

While they hemmed and hawed around, I went to the desert and played in the Palm Springs Open, a LPGA tournament held at Tamarisk Country Club. I loved it there! I wrote Stanford a letter and said that a doctor had advised me to live in a desert climate, so I wouldn't be coaching their golf team. I passed up the Stanford job — can you believe that?

During the tournament I had thought, "Boy, this is a neat place. I'd sure like to live and teach here in the winter." I went to the office and asked how to apply for a teaching job at the club.

"Well," said the receptionist, "the board is meeting just over there in that room. I'll see if they'll talk to you." I was invited into their meeting. One of the board members was Tom May from the May Company, and one was Nathan Ohrbach from Ohrbach's Department Store. Both were prominent merchants in the Los Angeles area. At that time, the board hired the pros, not the management.

1955. Shirley's business card from Fox Hills Country Club.

I said, "My name is Shirley Spork. I have my teaching credential from Michigan State Normal College. I am an established player and a teacher, and I would like to come here to teach in the winter."

"How much would you have to make?" they asked.

"Well, I have to eat just like you do. It could rain every day so you'd have to guarantee me 'x' number of dollars per month."

I left Ukiah at the end of 1954 and headed to the Los Angeles area. I played in a few tournaments and then got a full-time teaching position at Fox Hills Country Club in Culver City at the beginning of 1955. I wasn't there very long before being hired at Tamarisk Country Club for their fall season. Finally, I had ended up at the club where I had wanted to teach at after playing in the LPGA

73

tournament two years earlier.

That tournament, the Palm Springs Open, was the first LPGA event that Helen Lengfeld sponsored in Southern California. It was in April of 1953. Our Tour numbers were still small, so we went out to the local clubs and recruited golfers to expand our field. We asked all the women amateurs with a handicap of 10 or less to play in the tournament. It increased our numbers and brought the locals out to watch. Jackie Pung, reigning U.S. Women's Amateur Champion, won it that year.

Back when I interviewed with the Tamarisk Board, they agreed to pay me "x" number of dollars a month if it rained, but they never had to because I made enough teaching. On the days I taught, I was given a meal at the club for free. Tamarisk also paid my health insurance year-round, even in the summer when I was out playing the LPGA Tour. The job was my security blanket.

I got paid once a month. Ellsworth Vines, who was the head pro, would use our money during the month and "invest" it. I'd have to ask him two or three times for my paycheck.

He would say, "Oh you don't really need it, do you?"

I would tell him, "Yes, I do!"

Teaching was my fallback. I could leave in the summers and play on the LPGA Tour knowing I had a steady job waiting for me in the fall. This is not the best way to compete on the Tour. Your game isn't very sharp. I was teaching all winter and trying to play in the summer. It was tough competing against the year-round players.

I played with two different sets of clubs; one in the winter and another in the summer. My summer clubs had a heavier swing weight.

One of the Tamarisk members owned the Ojai Valley Inn Golf Course near Santa Barbara. He asked if I would consider being the head pro. He said he first needed to check with Ellsworth Vines, and asked if I was okay with that. Ellsworth was a past president of the Southern California PGA and the head pro who I was working for at Tamarisk. Ellsworth said he didn't think I should be the pro. "We need to give the job to one of our men members," he said.

I lost that job because I was a woman. That was in 1956. The owner wanted me to be the pro but was talked out of it. That's the only time I've ever had any trouble with jobs and the PGA. They ended up hiring Harry Pressler who taught Mickey Wright. He wasn't there very long, only about a year-and-a-half.

I had worked at Tamarisk for five years when Joe Blumenfeld asked me to open and manage a new course. He was a Tamarisk founding member and had made his wealth from movie theaters and bowling alleys in Northern California. Joe and some partners had just finished building Tanforan Golf Course in San Bruno near San Francisco. They built it in the middle of the Tanforan Race Track which was one of the oldest racetracks in California.

Louis (Lou) Boyer was another Tamarisk board member. He was a very wealthy real estate developer. Lou befriended me and became my first and only financial backer. He said, "You'll need some money to stock your pro shop." He gave me his business card and told me to go to his office on Wilshire Boulevard in Los Angeles.

When I arrived, his secretary said, "Here's the check." I had asked for $10,000, but when I looked at the check, it was for $50,000! She told me that Mr. Boyer said it would take all of that to stock my shop. Lou took a chance on me, and I was relieved when I finished paying back his generous loan. I certainly couldn't have chosen a better financial backer.

Lou was not a young man when we met. He hit balls on the range and only played an occasional round because of his age. When I had a break, Lou would sit on the driving range with me and chat about anything and everything. He was killing time until his buddies walked off the 18th green and he could join them for lunch and cards. You would have never guessed about his enormous wealth.

Lou's wife, Mae, suffered with severe arthritis. She was bedridden, and I would go visit her. They lived a few blocks from Tamarisk. Lou opened a clinic for arthritis patients in his wife's name. It was in Los Angeles and free to everyone since Lou bankrolled it all. Years later, after his wife died, Lou became a close friend of Israel's Prime Minister, Golda Meir.

Tanforan was a 9-hole executive course with a lake in the middle. There were two 4-pars and seven 3-pars. The 3-pars ran from 110 to 168 yards. We also had a big driving range with over 40 hitting stations.

There were two other similar courses in the San Francisco

area. One was in San Mateo (Bay Meadows) and one in Berkeley (Golden Gate Fields). They too were built in the middle of race tracks. I don't believe any of these three courses are still open. We used to run the track for exercise which was a mile and a quarter and had quite a pitch.

The PGA pros in my area were very supportive. They even put on clinics to help get the word out that our driving range at Tanforan was open at night.

Next to the track was the See's Candy factory. It was across the street from the green on the first hole. I smelled See's Candy all day, every day!

Across the street was the Golden Gate National Cemetery which was a military cemetery.

Tanforan Race Track was used as a military training center in World War I and a Japanese-American internment camp during World War II. They used the horse stalls to house the people who had been rounded up. The track had quite a history.

At first, my office was in the tote board because we were building the golf shop. The wind rattled the openings where the odds were posted, and mice ran around my feet. It was colder than cold with the wind and fog coming off the San Francisco Bay. I had the heater on, boots on, a scarf on, and a coat on, but still never could get warm.

It took a few months to build my pro shop behind the tote board. I designed the shop so that all the storage was under the counters. I had an office, bag storage, club rental, and a shower. We also built a snack bar behind the tote board with six stools and three booths. There was a sink in a closet and a stainless-steel fryer. The restrooms were around the corner.

"Little Nick" worked for me. I bought him an inflatable bed so he could stay there. It gave him a chance to get on his feet. He was a great help to me as we worked to get the course up and running.

San Francisco was very unionized. I could be the janitor six days a week, but on the seventh day, we had to have a union janitor. All he did was empty the wastebaskets and mop the floors, but this satisfied the union. Our greens superintendent had to belong to the Gravediggers Union because they didn't have one for greenskeepers. On Sunday, which was his day off, I could change the cup on the greens because I was the manager.

One time I wanted to put in a French drain down one of the fairways. A French drain is where you dig a ditch and put rocks in it. I asked our greenskeeper to go and rent a trencher. He drove it back and wasn't on it more than 10 minutes when the union boss came over from the horse barn and asked if he had a permit to drive that piece of equipment. He didn't, so he had to get off, and I got on. I didn't know how to run it, but I started it up, and the union boss left. After that, the greenskeeper got back on, and we finished the ditch. It was rather silly, but we worked around all the rules.

When the cars came in off the 101 highway at sunup, I was there to unlock the main gate of the race track.

Our course was close to several offices. At lunchtime, people would buy a sandwich from our snack bar, play nine holes, and head back to work.

The wind blew really hard off the San Francisco Bay. We were open at night, so I put up a canvas next to the range to help block the wind.

We couldn't be open during race season because of the chance that a ball might land on the track and injure a horse. When we closed for the race season, which was twice a year, I had to take all the canvas down. I took those few weeks off and headed back to my home in Palm Desert for a much-needed break.

The Bing Crosby National Pro-Amateur Golf Tournament was held each year at Pebble Beach Golf Links. It was about a two-and-a-half hour drive from Tanforan. In January 1962, the tournament experienced some terrible weather. It rained and even snowed. Can you believe that it actually snowed at Pebble Beach? They postponed the final round until Monday which was lucky for me. I had Mondays off, so I drove to Pebble Beach to watch.

As I was walking in, Maury DeMots came running up to me and said, "I need you! I need you to sit on the 18th tee and record what's happening around the course. Bing Crosby is going to be reporting the action on TV. He'll stand behind you. You need to feed him the latest updates you hear on the walkie-talkie." Maury was one of our early teaching members and worked for the American Broadcasting Company (ABC). She was the first woman to direct a national golf telecast when she headed up this tournament for the studio in 1960.

I went out and sat at a table looking at the 18th tee and the beautiful Pacific Ocean. It brought back memories of the special shot I had hit from the ocean years ago when I played Pebble Beach in the Weathervane Tournament.

The 17th green was just behind me. I listened to what was being said on the walkie-talkie and passed that information on to Bing so he could report it on TV. Information like; how many golfers were under par, who sank a putt, and who was coming next. I spent the entire day sitting there. I never saw a shot on the course, but I knew what every player was doing.

Soon after my trip to Pebble Beach, one of the owners brought his son in to manage Tanforan. I would leave to play in a tournament, and he would invite all his friends over. They would use all the rental sets and my equipment. The "manager" would give away my supplies as gifts. I went to the owners and said, "I can't work with this guy. I have a contract, and you are not holding up your end of the bargain." They didn't agree, so we parted ways. I managed the course for two years from January 1961 to October 1962.

When I was head pro at Tanforan, we had to work around the accreditation rules for a PGA Apprentice. A young man working as my assistant couldn't receive credits in the PGA program. Their bylaws said that an apprentice had to work for a Class "A" PGA professional. A Class "A" **LPGA** professional wasn't acceptable. When

I had a PGA apprentice working for me who needed to earn his credits, I'd wine and dine the local PGA pros. I would take them to dinner, and send them gifts so they would make sure my apprentice received his points. They gave the credits under the table. They agreed that what I was doing was the right thing, but according to their bylaws, it wasn't allowed.

Back in the 1950s, Goldie Bateson was the first woman head pro in Wisconsin. She ran New Berlin Hills Golf Course and had the same problem. Young men who wanted to work through the PGA program could only get credits working for a PGA professional. They couldn't get credits working for a woman head pro.

Dr. Gary Wiren was the Director of Education for the PGA from 1972 to 1980. He was responsible for getting that changed. He got it passed that an apprentice working for a **LPGA** head pro could earn his PGA credits. This was very helpful for the few women pros who were running golf facilities and created a good relationship between the PGA and the LPGA.

Soon after I left Tanforan, I played in the LPGA Championship at Stardust Country Club in Las Vegas, Nevada and finished second. Woo-hoo! Then I went back to Palm Springs, but instead of teaching at Tamarisk, I went to Indian Wells Country Club.

In May 1964, I was offered the head pro job at a brand new course in Warren, Vermont, called Sugarbush. It was the perfect summer job since it ran from Memorial Day to Columbus Day. It was a 16-week job which was a very short season. They closed for the winter.

Joakim Lehmkuhl had built a ski resort called Sugarbush which was managed by his daughter. She later married a golfer, and they decided to build an 18-hole golf course at the bottom of the hill. They hired me to run their new course.

Joakim had an interesting life. He came to America in 1940 leaving his native homeland, Norway, just before the Nazi invasion. He was grateful to be safe and wanted to help his new country in the war effort. Joakim was a clock maker, and he started a company called United States Time Corporation. They made fuse timers for the defense department. In 1969, the company he had started during the war was renamed. The new name was . . . Timex!

The designer of Sugarbush Golf Course was Robert Trent Jones, Sr. His team surveyed the land in the winter on snow skis. They didn't understand that under the snow was solid bedrock. When summer came, and the crew started to build the course, they had to blast through all this rock to create some of the holes in the way they had been designed. The second hole was mostly rock. There were spots throughout the course where rock would just stick up in the fairway. They chose not to blast anymore since it cost too much money. Building the course was so expensive that they could only afford the first nine holes that year.

Here was a case where the owners should have sued the architect. They paid the architect to design the course, but because it was surveyed in the snow, no one knew about all the rock. It's a good

1964. Head Pro Shirley in the golf shop at
Sugarbush Golf Course, Warren, Vermont.

thing the owners had lots of money because building the course was very, very expensive.

Former PGA Tour player Gene Sarazen came to play one time. He was checking to see about using our course for *Shell's Wonderful World of Golf.* This was a wildly popular TV show which featured two professional golfers playing an 18-hole match. These stroke-play challenges were held on different courses throughout the world. Interestingly enough, the first three-golfer challenge was held in 1969 in Bangkok, Thailand, and featured Sandra Haynie, Carol Mann, and Kathy Whitworth. When Mr. Sarazen came to check out our course, I wanted to tell him how to play our second hole because there was only one way to play it. It was a blind hole, and you had to hit a two iron off the tee. If you hit a driver, you would lose your ball. He didn't want to listen to me. He went out and played it, got into trouble, and then didn't approve of having the show filmed at our course because of that hole.

When I worked at Sugarbush, I had this whole big chalet to myself. It could sleep 20 people! Four bedrooms, each with double beds — you know how ski chalets are — and right on the golf course. I invited all my friends to come and play golf, and they had a place to stay.

I was the cook, maintained the carts, and ran the pro shop. I did everything. There were a couple of young boys from a farm down the road who rode their bikes over to help me. We had gas carts, and I wore the key to the gas tank around my neck. Nobody had a key but me. We also had to put oil in the carts. Some of the ski bums helped me because it was their off season, but I had to be careful they didn't help themselves to my supplies. I took a day off once and the next morning found all sorts of stuff missing.

The clubhouse was a century-old dairy farmhouse. The barn was connected to the house because with the snow in the winter, the farmers had to have easy access to their cattle. I used the area where the cows had been to store my golf carts. I took out one of the walls and made counters for a shop area. I put orange Formica on them which looked really nice with the gray barn wood. On the walls, I put Masonite pegboard up so I could hang stuff. There was an old

*1960s. The Sugarbush Golf Course clubhouse
was a converted farmhouse. Warren, Vermont.*

chest left there, so I put socks in it and displayed shirts above it. I
moved a window seat that was in the attic down to the shop. It was a
bench that had sides on it and was the size of the window. It was an
antique, and I used it as part of my display.

We made a coffee shop area in another room in the farmhouse. I had a counter, a two-burner electric hot plate, and a toaster
oven. That's how I cooked. I didn't have a fry station or an oven. I
would make open-faced sandwiches in the toaster oven. I had a pot
on my hot plate that held 12 cups of soup or chili. I'd be making
chili, and the guys would come in and say, "Oh, you're making chili?
Put my name on the list." I could only make 12 cups, so that's what

I sold.

The course didn't have a liquor license, so I would go to the ABC Store which was a state liquor store. Alcohol was really cheap in Vermont, and I would stock my own bar for the locals who played. They would make their own drink and put some money in the tip jar. When we ran out of something, I would take the tip money and replace it. We just didn't record that we sold any.

In the fall, I would head back home to the California desert, but I only worked at Sugarbush for two summers before accepting a full-time job with the National Golf Foundation (NGF).

I taught at Indian Wells Country Club for 15 winters before the owners of Tamarisk Country Club asked me to come back and work for them. Johnny Revolta, Tamarisk's head pro, had left to work at Mission Hills Country Club. It was hard breaking the news that I was leaving to the people who I'd come to love at Indian Wells but opportunities seldom come along like that. I left Indian Wells and taught at Tamarisk a second time.

Working in such an intense environment wore me out. It was just too demanding. I was giving 14 lessons a day. I showed up at the course early and gave my lesson list to the bag boy so he could bring everybody's clubs from bag storage out to the range. The student would arrive, take their lesson, and off they'd go. As soon as they walked away, the next one would be waiting. After I finished teaching, I wrote up all the lesson charges. It made for very long days.

Many of our members also belonged to Hillcrest, Brentwood,

and El Caballero Country Clubs which were all located in the Los Angeles area. I would work two weeks at Tamarisk and then take two days off. On my "days off," I'd head to Los Angeles and teach. I would give 15 lessons in a day, 30 lessons in two days, and then drive back home and start the process all over.

I taught at the Westwood Driving Range which was at Sawtelle and Wilshire Boulevards. It was a huge driving range with lots of teachers. To walk from where you signed in to where you were teaching was over a block. There must have been more than a hundred hitting stations. Now a big Veterans Healthcare Center building is there.

I stayed with my good friend, Jane Woolley, who lived close to the range. Jane would book my lessons so that when I arrived, I was all set. I also stayed with Jane and taught at the range during the summer months when it was too hot to teach in the desert. This allowed me to service my clientele year-round. I spent winters at Tamarisk and summers at the Westwood Driving Range.

Shirley visiting her mentor, Joey Rey,
when he was serving as the golf pro on a cruise ship.

Little Shirley and Big Shirley at Indian Wells Country Club.

I was a young girl aspiring to play the LPGA Tour when I first met Shirley. It was in the 1960s at Indian Wells County Club in Palm Springs, California. Shirley took me under her wing as she has with so many others; teaching, guiding, helping, and sharing her wealth of knowledge.

Shirley's middle name is "Golf." Shirley and I were co-leaders in the first round of the Dallas Civitan Open years ago which is a super great memory. Although I found greener pastures and strayed from the Tour life, our friendship did not stray.

We've had many fun times together like driving to Laughlin, Nevada, where we pulled over and cut wild asparagus with my pocket knife. Everywhere we traveled, we enjoyed wild berries, fruits, and other treats thanks to Shirl's eagle eye.

Spontaneous adventures were always an extra perk of traveling with Shirley. Anther time on our way to Laughlin Shirley said, "Pull over, stop, grab your driver, and some balls." Before you know it, we were hitting balls across the Colorado River.

No matter where we traveled, golf went with us. One trip we had rented a 58-foot long and 8-foot wide canal boat. We were cruising The Stratford-upon-Avon Canal and Shirley said, "Pull over and tie up." Over the fence we went with two partial sets of clubs. We played our way back to the golf shop, had a nice visit with the staff, played our way back to the boat, and cruised down the canal to a pub to enjoy a half-pint of Guinness.

Then there was the yacht trip where we jumped off and played The Belfry in England. Again, we each carried about six clubs. Shirley shot a 60 . . . another super-great memory.

I got to spend time with Shirley when she flew to Naples, Florida, in November 2015 to accept the Patty Berg Award. This award is presented by the LPGA to a person who "exemplifies diplomacy, sportsmanship, goodwill, and contributions to the game of golf." Congratulations Shirley! Thank you for your dedication to the game. I am very thankful for our many years of friendship.

Linda S. Galloway
LPGA Tour - Life Member

HOLE # 5

Traveling Further

From humble Michigan beginnings, the teacher/player found herself golfing at Pebble Beach with Bing Crosby. Then there was the wet and windy round at historic St Andrews, complete with a huge gallery. Or how about playing golf on television! These were all incredible opportunities for a young woman. Her adventures and education didn't end there. There was always more to learn and a host of invaluable experiences which Shirley would draw upon throughout her career.

Early in 1951, Joey Rey asked me to give a clinic at Pasatiempo Golf Club in Santa Cruz, California, during a Northern California Junior Girls Tournament. That's when I first met Helen Lengfeld who was a huge supporter of junior golf. She was also a financial and psychological "Godmother" to all of us during the early years of the LPGA Tour.

Helen was a wealthy woman from the San Francisco area. She was the chairperson for the United Voluntary Services (UVS), an organization she created to help veterans. Because of her love of golf, she established 9-hole courses at numerous veterans' hospitals across the country. Local women's clubs volunteered to go to these hospital courses and play golf with the recuperating vets. She visited every single one of the veterans' hospital in the United States and was well known in the military for her efforts.

Soon after I met Helen, she asked if I would like to come over and play Pebble Beach. She had a cottage there. Whew, of course I would! I had heard about Pebble Beach. I knew all about Pebble Beach. I had dreamed about playing Pebble Beach.

Back in September of 1948, the National Women's Amateur Golf Tournament was held at that famous course. I couldn't afford the trip from Michigan to California. I was offered a plane ticket, but couldn't accept because I would lose my amateur standing. I was disappointed but thought, "Someday I **will** get to play Pebble Beach." Now the time had finally come!

Helen said she would arrange it and find a place for me to stay. True to her word, the next day after the clinic, I drove behind her in the dark following these two little taillights in the fog. We drove through the entry gate of 17-Mile Drive and down the road; turning here and there, and finally we pulled in. I can remember hearing the gravel on the driveway.

She told me that a friend let her use his house, so I would be staying there. In the morning she would take me down and introduce me to the Pebble Beach head pro.

The following morning when I woke up, I walked over to the

window and pulled the drapes open. There I was on the first tee at Pebble Beach! I was right there, in the first house on the left! I was just shy of my 24th birthday and was able to play Pebble Beach for the first time all because of Helen's thoughtfulness and generosity.

I later found out I had spent the night at Lawson Little's house. He was a great amateur golfer. In fact, he was the first golfer to win both the British and the American Amateur Championships two years in a row back in the mid-1930s. Lawson later won several times as a pro, including the 1940 U.S. Open. He was inducted into the World Golf Hall of Fame in 1980, and I had spent the night in his house. I heard that Lawson's home was recently torn down to build several smaller cottages on the first hole of Pebble Beach.

Soon after my first round at Pebble Beach, I was able to play there again. Helen knew Samuel F.B. Morse, the owner of Pebble Beach, and arranged for one of the four legs of the Weathervane Tournament to be played there in 1950 and 1951. Marilynn Smith and I went out to play a practice round before the tournament started on May 5, 1951. We walked up to the 9th tee, and there sat Bing Crosby smoking his pipe. He had three clubs with him.

Marilynn said, in an excited whisper, "That's Bing Crosby — that's Bing Crosby!"

And I said, "Yes, Marilynn, that's Bing Crosby."

He asked, "Do you mind if I play a few holes with you?"

Marilynn couldn't believe it.

I said, "Sure, come on."

Bing played back to his home with us: 9, 10, 11, 12, and 13. His house was on the 13th hole looking out at the ocean. By then it was getting dark. He said, "Come on in. I'll fix you a Coke and then take you back to the clubhouse." Bing showed us into his den, and there was a customized Wurlitzer jukebox. The machine was at least six feet wide and seven feet tall. There were records on three rows. Each record was assigned a code. When a combination of buttons was punched, an arm went up, grabbed the record, took it down, and played it. I read all the titles, and not one of the records in the entire jukebox was his. Not one! We played a few records, and he told some stories.

Finally, Marilynn said it was time to go, and Bing offered to drive us back. We threw our clubs in the trunk and climbed into the car. As he drove along, Bing would press this button with his left foot. The button was on the floorboard, and it went ding-dong, ding-dong. It sounded just like a San Francisco cable car. I later heard that it was a gift from Joan Fontaine. Well after that ride, Marilynn and I knew we just had to find one of those ding-dong bells for our car floorboard, and we actually did.

I remember playing the par-five, 18th hole during one of the rounds in the Weathervane Tournament. I had hit a good drive, and a good second shot, but then pulled my third shot into the ocean. The ocean was played as part of the course. The tide was out, so I climbed down and hit my ball which was sitting right next to this big rock. It was a good shot, and my ball flew back up onto the fairway.

May, 1951. Shirley hitting out of the Pacific Ocean on the 18th hole of Pebble Beach Golf Links, LPGA Weathervane Tournament.

I holed my fifth shot from about 35 yards out for a par! Just goes to show you that there's more than one way to play a hole.

After I had walked off the 18th green, the cameraman said, "We would like you to replay that shot."

I asked him, "Why do you want me to replay it?"

"Well," he said sheepishly, "we didn't get it on film."

So I climbed back down to the ocean, looking smart in my kelly-green blouse and white skirt, to hit the shot again. When I got there, the tide was coming in, but we reenacted my "famous" shot, and it's archived out there somewhere. Hitting out of the Pacific Ocean on the 18th hole at Pebble Beach was a fun experience and a great memory!

Just as Helen Lengfeld was the West Coast "Godmother," Alvin Handmacher was our "Godfather" on the East Coast during the early days of the LPGA Tour. Alvin was in the clothing business and made a line of women's suits and sports clothes called *The Weathervane*. During the Tour's first four seasons, he put up money for tournaments in the North, South, East, and West just like the spokes on a weathervane.

The four tournaments were spread throughout the season which meant a lot of driving. The cities varied, but the last one was always on the East Coast because Alvin's office was in New York. Our scores were tallied from the four tournaments, and the player with the lowest overall combined score won an extra $5,000. That was big money back then! Babe Zaharias captured the first Weathervane purse in 1950, Patty Berg in 1951, Betsy Rawls in 1952, and Louise Suggs won the final year in 1953.

At the 1951 New York Weathervane Tournament it rained so hard that they suspended play on the final day. It was pouring! They rescheduled the final round for the following day. I was teaching school at Bowling Green State University and couldn't figure out

1951. Alice Bauer and Shirley,
New York Weathervane Tournament rain delay.

how I could stay over and play on Monday. I had to teach on Tuesday and needed Monday to travel.

We had all checked out of our motel that Sunday morning before heading to the course, so we were stuck! Helen Lengfeld had come to visit her good friend, Alvin, and to watch the tournament.

Several of us were standing around trying to figure out what to do when she walked up and said, "I have a suite. You all come up and stay with me." So eight or 10 of us went to Helen's Waldorf Astoria suite. Imagine that! They brought in roller beds and it was like a big slumber party.

After we got settled, Helen said she was too tired to head down to the dining room and that she'd just order room service. It wasn't long before there was a knock on the door. When Helen opened the door, several carts were rolled into the middle of the room, and each plate was covered with a beautiful silver dome. That was a first for many of us. Helen had ordered enough food to feed a small army. Somehow, she must have known we were all hungry. It was like having a smorgasbord right there in our room as we filled our plates with a taste from each of the delicious dishes.

Looking back, I'm sure she knew that, even though we were starving, most of us couldn't afford to eat at The Waldorf. It was all we could do to scrounge up enough money to pay for the mandatory valet parking. If it hadn't been for Helen, I suspect that some of us would have spent the night in our cars, cold and wet. What could have been a disaster turned into a wonderful, entertaining evening. We were given the opportunity to spend quality time and get to know each other better, thanks to Helen.

The entire weekend was a fun experience. It started with our round of golf on Saturday, getting drenched on Sunday, and Marilynn driving from the course through a tunnel in stop and go traffic.

We had trouble finding the hotel, but finally, we got to spend an unforgettable night at the famous Waldorf Astoria Hotel. We were just "babes in the woods."

Because it was so wet, they actually weren't able to reschedule the final round until Wednesday, so I wasn't able to play. After that final round, Babe and Patty were tied. Four tournaments spread across the entire country, and they had the same combined score!

About two weeks later, they arranged for Babe and Patty to meet again in a two-day, 36-hole playoff to decide the winner of the Weathervane. Patty shot a 75 on the final 18-holes to beat Babe by one stroke. That was quite a finish and earned Patty the extra $5,000 for the 1951 Weathervane competition. Imagine ONE shot being worth that much money!

Helen and Alvin were good friends and extremely generous to us. They both were Jewish, and each had their own charity. Helen's was the United Voluntary Services (UVS), and Alvin's was the Damon Runyon Cancer Memorial Fund. The Runyon Fund was one of the first national charities for cancer. It was founded by Walter Winchell after Damon died of cancer in 1946. Damon was a well-known newspaper reporter. He covered sports and general news and also wrote several short stories. The musical *Guys & Dolls* was based on two of those stories. We played a lot of charity events for the Damon Runyon Cancer Fund.

Then there was George S. May who owned a management consultant firm and was also a huge supporter of both men's and

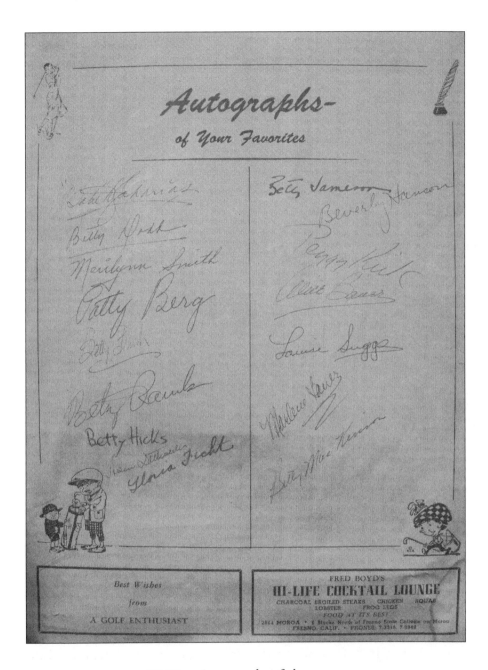

1950s. Autographs of the greats.

women's golf. His was one of the first companies in the Midwest that conducted factory surveys to look for inefficiencies. George also owned the Tam O'Shanter Golf Course in Niles, Illinois. He put on a tournament called the All-American Open from 1941 through 1957. I played in it first as an amateur and then as a pro a few years later. I won the amateur division in 1948.

A few years after starting the All-American Open, George started another tournament that he named the World Champion-ship of Golf. The two tournaments were usually held back to back in August. The format was match play for amateurs and stroke play for professionals.

In the All-American Open, everyone wore numbers safe-ty-pinned on their backs. There were men pros, lady pros, men ama-teurs, lady amateurs, and international players. Sports celebrities, like Joe Lewis, also played. Johnny Bulla, who was a professional, would play nine holes right-handed and the other nine holes left-handed. It seemed like every golfer in the world played. It was a big, big tourna-ment. Play started when the sun came up and continued until it got dark. Sometimes the players who teed off late couldn't finish their round. So the following morning they would pick up where they had left off.

The World Championship was the first tournament shown live on television. It was 1953 and they televised the 18th green. George had bleachers built around the green as an extra treat for Tam O'Shanter members who might find themselves on television when the camera panned the crowd. The American Broadcasting Company (ABC) agreed to broadcast one hour of each round after George paid them $32,000. On the final day, Lew Worsham holed a wedge from about 140-yards out for an eagle to beat Chandler Harper and win $25,000. That shot was shown live to a national audience by a single camera located above the grandstand on the 18th green. It was estimated that over a million people witnessed that great finish thanks to George and ABC.

We all knew they were going to film the 18th green. We also knew that we were playing to a live audience since George had built the bleachers around the green. For weeks we thought about what we were going to wear, even though it was obviously filmed in black and white. We thought about how we were going to look and we dieted.

We were obsessed with the 18th hole! The north branch of the Chicago River flowed through the course and cut across the fairway right in front of the 18th green. The green was elevated with big yawning trees surrounding it. At that time, if you hit a good drive and your ball was sitting up, you could hit a five wood, carry it over the river, between the trees, and onto the green. We all wanted to perform our best for the camera. We just prayed that we'd hit a good drive, have a good lie, and hit our approach shot onto the green.

The first day I hit a good drive and my second shot landed on the green. I was so excited. I walked across the bridge, and to make sure I was on television, I walked the long way around the green to mark my ball. On the first tee, they had given us bingo markers which were just flat, little plastic markers without a peg. Since my ball was closer to the hole than my opponent's, I bent down and placed the plastic marker behind it. I picked up my ball and then tapped the marker down with my putter.

I walked all the way around the green and over to the other side, once again making the most of my television fame. My opponent was walking back and forth. I thought she was spending a long time studying her putt but she finally putted out. As she stroked her putt, I looked down and there was my bingo marker stuck on the underside of my putter. I thought, "What do I do now? Make a big scene or just forget it?" I casually walked back, like I knew where it was, placed the ball down, pretended to pick up the marker and put it in my pocket, putted, and walked off the green. I wouldn't have gotten by with that today with the television coverage.

My opponent said, "Geez, I hope I didn't step in your line, I couldn't find your marker."

"No problem," I said. "There was no way you could have seen it since it was right here on the end of my putter!"

The next day when I played the 18th hole, I hit the green again. My opponent had hit her ball on the fringe close to where you walked off the bridge. I was so busy looking at the camera that after I crossed the bridge, I accidentally stepped on her ball. I stepped on it! On national television! The reporter said, "Wow! These women are sure competitive!"

George really helped promote the whole game of golf with

those tournaments even though they were crazier than a three-ringed circus. In fact, the *Saturday Evening Post* called them, "a cross between a country fair and a good airplane crash." They were held for quite a few years and were good exposure for competition at all phases of the game including pros, amateurs, men, women, and juniors. The tournaments came to an end in 1958 when George had a rift with the PGA.

Speaking of early television in golf, there was a program called *All-Star Golf.* Two top PGA professionals would play a match against each other. The program ran from 1957 to 1963 and was filmed at various golf courses across the nation. In 1958, five of the programs were filmed in the Palms Springs area. The first one was played at O'Donnell Golf Club. O'Donnell's had nine holes and was the first golf course built in the Coachella Valley back in the 1920s. The next two episodes were at Tamarisk Country Club where I taught. The final two were filmed at Thunderbird Country Club which was the first 18-hole course built in the area. The competition was filmed by one camera mounted on a truck. The truck would follow the players hole by hole. The crew could get about six holes on tape per day, so it took three days or more to film the entire match. It was very interesting to watch the process.

I was sponsored by Golfcraft and also endorsed A.E. Penfold Golf Company golf balls. They were a British ball manufacturer. In the fall of 1951, Mr. Dick Penfold, son of the company founder, was in the States and I got to play nine holes with him and Mr. Woolley

CUNARD WHITE STAR
TO EUROPE

NAME _Shirley Spork_

SHIP _Queen Elizabeth_

SAILING DATE _Sept. 27_

SAILING FROM _N.Y. Pier #90_

SAILING TO _Southampton_

CLASS _Cabin_ | DECK | STATEROOM NUMBER

WANTED ☒
IN STATEROOM | MARK X | _C_ | _162_

NOT WANTED ☐
DURING VOYAGE | MARK X

September 27, 1951. Shirley's cabin assignment aboard the Queen Elizabeth on her trip to Europe.

(the owner of Golfcraft). I shot a 30 which was six under par. I had seven birdies and a three-putt bogey. Mr. Penfold asked if I would like to go to England, Scotland, Wales, and France to give clinics for his company. I said, "Sure, why not?" I was 24 years old, out of college, and teaching at Bowling Green State University in Ohio.

When planning my trip, Mr. Penfold asked me what I wanted to do while I was in Europe. I could think of only one thing . . . and that was to play St Andrews! Not as an exhibition, I just wanted to play that famous links course.

Mr. Woolley's daughter, Jane, traveled with me as my manager. Mr. Penfold met us as we walked off the Queen Elizabeth in Southampton, England, and rode with us on a train to Edinburgh, Scotland. The next morning the Penfold sales representative took us to St Andrews.

I had dreamed of playing the course by myself, but Mr. Penfold had arranged for me to be paired with the 1950 St Andrews University captain. We played against the man who had beaten Bing Crosby in the 1950 British Amateur and an ex-Royal Air Force (RAF) champion. All of a sudden, it was a match.

Prior to leaving for the trip, I knew it was going to be cold. My mentor, Joey Rey, had told me to buy three sweaters in sizes 34, 36, and 38. He said, "You put one right over the other. When you play in the rain, you'll be warm, but you'll still be able to swing." We didn't have rain gear back then.

It was really cold and damp the day we played. Jane had on an overcoat and even she was freezing. While I was playing, she decided to head into town and buy some insulated underwear.

The four of us teed off. At the 1st hole, we had three spectators. At the 3rd hole, there were about 50. By the 8th hole, there were 100, and by the 16th and 17th, there were 200 to 300 following us. I thought, "Where did all these people come from?"

Jane finally caught back up with us on the course and said, "I couldn't buy anything because every shop is closed. They all have a sign on their door: 'American lady pro at links.'" All the owners had closed their shops to come out and watch me play, and anyone who

1951. Playing a match with British champions at St Andrews.

had gone into town to shop also ended up at the course.

Toward the end of the round, Jane said, "You better do something to entertain this crowd."

So when I got on the 18th tee box, I pulled an extra-long tee out of my golf bag. It was three inches long. I said, "On Sunday morning after you've had a few nips the night before, this is how you tee up your ball." I teed several balls up really high and hit a few trick shots for them.

It was after that when the captain said, "Would you like to come into the clubhouse?" In the U.S., the person who runs a clubhouse is called a general manager. Over there he's called a captain.

The captain invited me into the Royal and Ancient Office which is in the Royal and Ancient Clubhouse and we walked right in the front door. The front door! Until then, women were **not** allowed through this entrance.

All the way down the hall were these clubs hanging from top to bottom on the walls. Over the years, it had been the Royal & Ancient's job to test each new golf club that was submitted and decide if it was legal or illegal to use in competition. All the ones they deemed "illegal" were confiscated and hung on the walls. Many were extremely old and most looked very odd.

Earlier in the day, while we were playing the course, the men were intrigued that I could hit a wedge up in the air and make it sit softly on the green like a butterfly with sore feet. Most of the time they played in the wind, so they had learned to hit the ball low. The group of men who had followed us into the clubhouse wanted to know how I hit this high pitch shot, so someone handed me a club. I was just getting set to show them when the captain said, "No, no, no! Get up on the table so we can see better."

So I climbed up on this beautiful table, which seated about 20 people, in the boardroom of the Royal and Ancient and showed them how I hit a flop shot. I made sure to hit my invisible ball "thin" and not take a divot. After I swung, I was so relieved that I hadn't scuffed that gorgeous table! A writer from the *London Times* was there taking notes while I was doing all this.

*1951. The gallery watching Shirley play an exhibition
in Birmingham, England.*

After the demonstration was over, the captain asked, "Would
you like to see the men's locker room?"

And I thought, "Oh wow, this is really something." If you
look at a picture of the clubhouse, there's a window that looks

right out on the 1st tee. That's the locker room window. We walked through two swinging doors into a room that was filled with over-stuffed chairs. Along the wall were 30 to 40 lockers with brass plates, about 12 inches long and three inches high, each engraved with a member's name. When someone died the next guy in line would get that locker. Men were sipping their glasses of sherry, puffing on cigars, and looking out to see who was playing. When I walked in there, this older gentleman jumped up and almost keeled over to see a woman in the men's locker room at St Andrews.

Jane and I stayed at a pub in the town of St Andrews. There were four to six rooms for rent upstairs and the pub was downstairs. It wasn't a roadhouse because it was right in the middle of town. A lot of little towns had pubs like this. They had two bars — a public bar, and a private bar. Travelers and locals stopped in at the public bar while guests staying upstairs could go to the private bar.

One of the golfers I had played with earlier in the day, J.K. Wilson, was a building contractor. He had asked where we were staying and we had given him the name of the pub. He said he had something to give me to remember my visit. The pub was packed that evening because people knew we were staying there. Instead of spending a nice, quiet evening at the private bar, Jane and I had decided to meet and greet the locals at the public bar. Mr. Wilson showed up as promised and brought me this club which he had found inside the wall of a house he had torn down. It's called an A. (which stands for Alexander) Patrick Long Nose, made in the 1870s.

*1951. Shirley representing the A.E. Penfold Golf Ball Company
on her exhibition tour in Europe.*

It's one of the clubs in my collection that I highly treasure.

Although it was an experience to play there, St Andrews wasn't what I had expected. On a dry, calm day you can just top the ball and it rolls forever. However, it's rarely dry or calm. The wind is always blowing, or it's raining, or it's cold. They don't have many sunny, calm days. That's what makes St Andrews the gem it is.

Later on the trip, we toured London. There were still bombed out areas in the city that hadn't been rebuilt. Most of the office where Mr. Penfold had worked was destroyed. Only the reception area was left!

Mr. Penfold's father, A.E. Penfold, had started the golf ball company in England in 1930. The golf business was booming in the United States, so six years later he opened a factory in Brooklyn, New York. Mr. Penfold was returning to England after a business trip in 1941. He was a passenger on a freighter that was attacked and sunk in the Irish Sea. There were no survivors, so Dick Penfold inherited his father's company at a very young age.

Jane and I had brought a large suitcase full of canned ham, nylon stockings, and tea from the States to share with our English hosts. Meat was still being rationed, even though it was six years after the war. New clothes, especially nylon stockings, were scarcer than hen's teeth. Mr. Penfold told the story of buying a raincoat after he returned from military duty. Before leaving the store, he paid them to dirty it up because you weren't supposed to have any new clothes.

I remember giving a clinic where they served a luncheon of jugged hare, which is a rabbit dish. They couldn't get meat, so they cooked what they could find. When we went to a cocktail party at someone's home, we gave them one of our canned hams. That was a real treat for them, and they were so happy to get it.

We gave stockings to Mr. Penfold's secretary. You'd think we had given her a sack of gold. In England, they didn't have nylon, only

October, 1951. Flyer announcing exhibition at Heysham Golf Club.
Northwest of London on the Irish Sea.

silk, and that was nearly impossible to get.

We took tea in tea bags, but they took the tea out of the bags. To them, the bags made their tea taste like paper. We should have brought loose tea, but we didn't know.

One night we were invited to the Penfold's home. He had two small boys. They had a teepee set up in the living room and the kids were playing in it. I thought that was odd since teepees seem more American than English. Mr. Penfold probably brought it home from one of his trips to the U.S. as a gift for his sons.

Another evening Jane and I went to a movie. They played "God Save the Queen." Everyone rose to their feet, so Jane and I stood up. After everyone was reseated, they started the film.

Jane decided she wanted some candy, so she went out to the lobby to get a Cadbury chocolate bar. The lady behind the counter said, "That will be one ration coupon."

Jane said, "I don't have any coupons, just cash."

"If you don't have a coupon, you can't have the candy."

The next day we went to the ration board and got a book for the remainder of our trip. Each week was stamped and we gave the food stamps we weren't going to use to people working at the Penfold office.

At the inn where we stayed, you could have tea, a broiled tomato, a herring, and cold toast the first morning. If you stayed two days, you could have an egg. It was a big deal to get an egg.

If you stopped at a roadside inn, you could buy a meat pie which was made from an old Welsh recipe. Back in the day, the miner's wives would take leftover stew, put it in some dough and bake it. It was made with pork, beef, or lamb and had lard in it. The pie was eaten cold, and I had to try one. I thought it was awful!

Our trip continued on to France and we played at Saint Cloud, which is a famous course in Paris. We had planned to visit the Louvre the next day, but it was closed. So, we decided to golf again.

*1930s. Famous Penfold golf ball mascot. Company founder,
A.E. Penfold, fashioned it after his son, Dick Penfold.*

I was a guest of the men's French PGA, and to call their office,
you used a phone at a store front. Jane and I were trying to call when
a U.S. soldier came in and said, "I bet you're having trouble. Let me
see the number. You have to take this number and find a match-
ing phone." There were two rows of phones. If the first three numbers were 320, you had to find the phone with those numbers. If
it was 408, you had to find the 408 phone. We finally found the
correct phone and called the PGA office. A woman answered and
spoke French, of course. We were trying to reach the head of the

115

French PGA but couldn't get our message through to this woman. We couldn't speak French and she wasn't about to speak English. It was unfortunate.

So, instead of golfing, we went to a movie starring Bing Crosby. The movie was in French with English subtitles. There was an usher who took us to our seats and then just stood there. After we sat down, we were trying to figure out why he hadn't left when we saw another person tip their usher. Well, we didn't know that it was their custom to tip the usher, but we quickly learned.

After the movie, we wanted to go to a restaurant for dinner. Nothing was in English, of course. To secure a cab you had to show the driver where you wanted to go. Some said it was too far, while others said it wasn't far enough. After four cabs, we finally got one to take us.

Mr. Penfold asked me to stay over after my exhibition tour and then go to Australia. I said, "Oh, I need to be home for Christmas." Dumb me! Looking back, it was still an exciting, fun trip for a couple of naive, young American girls.

Years later, Jane and I traveled to Ireland on vacation. There was a 9-hole course in Kenmare. We found that we could only play six holes if the tide was in and all nine if the tide was out. They had square greens and all the maintenance was a community project. The local golfers each took turns mowing the greens and collecting the fees that had been deposited in a box near the first tee. I love finding gems like that in my travels.

Without the founders' tireless work and passion in creating the LPGA Tour as well as the LPGA Teaching Division, I would not have had the opportunity to have the exceptional career I did as an LPGA educator. But my golf "life" story really begins with one of the founders, Shirley Spork. It is my pleasure to write a bit about Shirley and our friendship.

It was the summer of 1967 after my junior year as an undergraduate studying teacher education/physical education and I was a just starting to play golf. Unlike other sports I had participated in, I was really horrible at golf. A good friend of mine, who was an accomplished amateur golfer from Vermont, suggested that I attend a National Golf Foundation (NGF) clinic at the Elks Club in Montpelier, Vermont. Shirley Spork was the instructor. You could attend the morning or the afternoon sessions for $5.00 for five days! Needless to say, I attended both sessions; the morning as a student and the afternoon as an assistant to the teacher — Shirley's "Go-fer!"

It was Shirley who saved me from giving up the game. It was Shirley who introduced me to teaching the game and the NGF education clinics. It was Shirley who recommended me to the NGF so I could become part of the education consultant/clinician staff. She drilled the short game shots during my lessons with her and encouraged me when the time was right to join the LPGA Teaching Division (now the LPGA Teaching and Club Professionals). That was after helping me lower my handicap to a single digit.

After many years of teaching and coaching at the college level, and earning my LPGA Class "A" status in the teaching division, I became Director of Education for the LPGA, my dream job. I oversaw the certification program for the LPGA Teaching and Club Professionals, a program that Shirley helped to establish for the LPGA in 1959. My career at the LPGA continued and I eventually became the Vice President of Professional Development.

Since my undergraduate days and throughout my professional career, Shirley has been a mentor. She is a teacher who not only helped me to become a respectable amateur golfer, but also a golf educator: teaching teachers to teach the fundamentals while keeping the game simple and fun. That's what leads to success in this great game.

Over the past almost 50 years, we have been unconditional "friends through golf." We have taught together, learned together at many seminars and clinics, played golf together, and have enjoyed traveling together to Solheim Cup competitions in the United States, Sweden, and Ireland.

I am truly grateful and honored to call Shirley Spork my mentor and friend.

Betsy Clark, PhD
LPGA Teaching & Club Professional - Class "A" Life Member
Former LPGA Vice President of Professional Development

Back in 1965, I attended my first LPGA National Golf School at Bowling Green State University which was near my home in Ohio. Leading this school was someone named, Shirley Spork. "Quite the in-charge person," I thought. I would go on to discover the wealth and experience behind that name based upon her great dedication to the game we both loved so much.

Shirley became a mentor, along with another masterful teacher, Ellen Griffin, during my early years with the National Golf Foundation. Teaching teachers how to initiate and strengthen golf in our nation's schools was our main mission in those years. What a privilege it was to learn from these and other legends of golf education. It was often said of us, "We had the best jobs in golf."

Shirley's wisdom and leadership equipped us all for bettering our careers in golf. We formed a professional friendship as experiences of giving countless clinics, workshops, and national seminars for teach-ers and coaches across the country became sprinkled with memories never to be forgotten.

At one point I acquired the nickname, "Pitch," from Shirley. She noticed I needed lessons in articulation, as I repeatedly referred to a "pitcher" of the golf swing instead of "picture!" I can still hear Shir-ley calling me, "Hey, Pitch!" Shirley's humor endeared her to us all.

So on this special occasion of your very own book, we say, "Our hats are off to you, Shirley!" Thank you for coming into our lives to en-

rich them whether we were on or off the course. Enjoy now the rewards of your lifelong giving to others, and to the advancement of this great game of golf. We love you!

Lorraine Abbott
LPGA Teaching & Club Professional - Master Life Member
National Golf Foundation (NGF) - Former Director of Education

HOLE # 6

Teaching Teachers

How many children know what they want to be when they "grow up?" Purchasing a putter at age 12, Shirley started chasing her dream. Slowly and methodically the Detroit native worked to master this game called golf. Who would have guessed that a young woman, living in the apartment above her, would factor so prominently in Shirley's future? How a loan, taken out on furniture, could instill a love for teaching and create a whole new career choice for generations to come.

In the 1950s the LPGA Tour members voted on everything at our annual meeting. One motion that surfaced several times was for the creation of a teaching division. It was voted down three years in a row because the members felt our organization was too small. They feared that neither division would survive if we split up. Marilynn Smith was President in 1959. It came down to her vote. Her deciding vote finally brought the LPGA Teaching Division into existence. So, that taught me **one** vote certainly **can** make all the difference!

With my education background, I instantly knew just how

historic Marilynn's vote could be for the future of women's golf.

I remember telling the girls, "Someday you're not going to be able to play the Tour anymore, and you're going to have to learn how to teach. You'll need to find a job." Many thought they would get a job because of their LPGA Tour fame. I told them, "You're nuts. You've got to have credentials. You can't just walk in and teach! You have to know how to teach. We have to teach women how to teach golf."

When we were just starting out in the 1940s and '50s, there were only a few key men who taught golf to women. Jerry Glynn was one. He was the head pro at Skycrest Country Club outside of Chicago before they hired Babe Zaharias in the spring of 1950. Tommy Armour in Florida was another, and there was Harry Pressler in California. I didn't think this was right. Women need to teach women. Men can't understand the differences in our swing or how we think.

I also felt we needed a system to teach our members how to handle group instruction and how to recognize error detection and correction. My passion was probably due to my degree in physical education where I had been taught how to teach sports to women.

We needed established and certified teachers. Most people thought anybody who was a golf pro was a teacher, too. But they weren't! People didn't know this, and unfortunately, many still don't. A person could take a lesson and not know if the teacher knew what they were talking about. All a golfer knew was that there was some person giving lessons at their club or local course. Anyone could hang up a shingle and say they were a golf pro, but they weren't certified as a professional teacher.

A teacher can do a lot of damage if they don't understand their pupil. Less is more! Sometimes we get too verbal and talk too much in a lesson. It's easy to overload a student. You get a student started, add a few too many swing thoughts, and they fall apart. Teachers have to be careful not to say too much.

The PGA certified its members to run a facility. Teaching wasn't their primary focus. The LPGA Teaching Division's vision was to certify women who could teach. Just because you can run a golf course doesn't make you a good instructor.

Barbara Rotvig, Betty Hicks, Marilynn, and I became founding members of the teaching division and served on the first teaching committee. Betty was appointed chairwoman, but her first love was aeronautics. She taught ground classes to pilots of all levels at Foothill Community College near San Francisco. This left her little time to devote to our new enterprise. Whenever she had a conflict, she would call and ask me to fill in for her.

In 1960 I was appointed committee chairwoman. We held the first LPGA National Golf School at the University of Michigan in Ann Arbor later that year. Barbara and I led it. Marilynn, Betty, Ellen Griffin, Mary Ann Reynolds, Jackie Pung, and Mary Lena Faulk volunteered to serve as our staff. It took a lot of women to staff these schools. The next school was also held in Ann Arbor, followed by two years at the University of North Carolina at Greensboro.

1961. Staff of the second National LPGA Golf School, University of Michigan, Ann Arbor. From left: Peggy Kirk Bell, Marilynn Smith, Barbara Rotvig, Patty Berg, Ellen Griffin, and Shirley.

Then we headed to the University of Vermont in Burlington while I was head pro at Sugarbush Golf Course. The last two years were held at Bowling Green State University where I had previously taught.

Our focus was teaching teachers how to teach. Our goal was to increase the number of teachers nationwide. In addition to improving their games, we wanted a standardized rating system for LPGA Teaching Professionals.

We offered the schools to women teaching at golf courses, physical education teachers, coaches, and just about any other woman interested in golf.

The golfers who attended the seminar were divided into groups. Each pro focused on a different part of the game: driving, putting, course management, and so on. The groups of students rotated around to the different stations. By doing this, those attending were also learning how to teach groups.

The programs were self-supporting. The local amateurs who signed up to attend the course would pay a fee. Those of us teaching would use that money to cover our expenses. After we had some success, the LPGA decided to get involved. They wanted us to send them expense receipts. We didn't bother with that. We just did our own thing.

We scheduled the schools at universities where I knew the head of the athletic department was a golfer. The sessions were held between Tour stops, and the LPGA players couldn't refuse to help us because the road to the next tournament went right past the college.

The players would stop by as they were driving to the next tournament and give a demonstration. Mickey Wright would say, "I'll come, but don't let them ask me any questions! I'll be there and do what you say, but don't ask me to talk!" Mickey didn't like to talk. It was hard for her, but she always came and demonstrated.

I would say, "Mickey, I want you to hit it right to left, or left to right, or this shot, or that shot." While she was demonstrating, I would explain to the students how she was creating the various ball flights. Once Mickey was done hitting shots, she'd get in her car and

*1962. Shirley teaching the LPGA National Golf School
at the University of North Carolina, Greensboro.*

go. Gone! Can you imagine having a front-row seat to watch one
of the greatest golfers who has ever played the game? I don't believe
most people appreciated what a privilege that truly was.

I also taught those who came to the school how to regrip
clubs. I bought some of those vices you screw onto the end of a table.
To this day people still come up to me and tell me how much they
appreciated me teaching them how to regrip a club. When the school
was held at Bowling Green State University, we used their inventory
of "Shirley Spork" signature clubs. The clubs were 10 years old by

then, but it didn't matter. I told them we would just regrip them. Everyone learned how to regrip clubs.

Besides the USGA, PGA, and LPGA, the other major organization was the National Golf Foundation (NGF). It was founded in 1936 by Joe and Herb Graffis. Their main focus was to promote the game of golf so the manufacturers could sell equipment. The two divisions of the NGF were: Course Development and Golf Education.

The NGF was supported by all the golf equipment companies. Each manufacturer had to pay the Foundation a set amount of money for each piece of equipment they sold. For instance, at that time, golf balls were three cents per dozen. If they sold a thousand dozen balls at three cents, they owed the NGF 30 dollars.

The NGF received requests from agencies, such as city recreation departments, about building golf courses. They would send out a rep if a city requested one, and the rep would run a study to see if building a course was feasible. The NGF Rep found out how many courses were in the city, how many people lived there, and how far a golfer had to drive to get to a course. Then they'd crunch the numbers and make recommendations. If a city was told that the local population could support another golf course, then they could start the process — like floating a bond to pay for construction.

There was a time when the government gave money to help encourage recreation. This was especially true throughout Texas and the Midwest. A farmer could take a piece of his land and put up a building. It had to have a restaurant on one side, a clubhouse on the

1964. Shirley hits the first shot at the opening of the Bowling Green State University Golf Course, Bowling Green, Ohio.

other side, and connected in the middle by a breezeway. That started the process of having a course built. Soon you owned a golf course, almost entirely paid for by the taxpayers.

Ellen Griffin was the driving force of the NGF Education Division in the 1960s. She had earned her teaching credential at Woman's College of the University of North Carolina, now known as the University of North Carolina at Greensboro (UNCG) in 1940. Ellen went on to earn her master's degree at UNC (Chapel Hill) and then joined the faculty of UNCG's Physical Education Department. She was a professor there until she retired in 1968.

While teaching at UNCG, Ellen helped form the Women's

Professional Golf Association (WPGA), so she was no stranger to golf. That was in 1944, along with Hope Seignious and Betty Hicks.

The NGF hired Ellen in 1962 while she was on sabbatical from UNCG. They wanted her to update the written materials and visual aids for their educational division to be used in our nation's public schools. Ellen traveled around the country instructing college teachers and coaches on how to teach golf. Eventually, she invited some of these attendees to become NGF Consultants to service their respective regions. Ellen also conducted clinics for the NGF. She was an expert at large group instruction.

After running the national seminar for a couple of years, she called me. It was 1966 while I was the head pro at Sugarbush Golf Course in Vermont. She said, "My sabbatical at the university is about up. I'm heading back to Greensboro. I want you to take over my job at NGF." I didn't think I wanted to do that. She said she was recommending Lorraine Abbott and me and that the NGF should divide the country — Lorraine would take the eastern half, and I would take the western half. So that's what we did, but trying to follow Ellen's lead was a daunting task.

Lorraine was teaching at the University of Illinois at Urbana-Champaign and resigned to take the full-time position with the NGF. We both started in 1966. I worked for the NGF for seven years until 1973 and Lorraine worked for them one year beyond that.

I remember Lorraine saying that she'd met Ellen at a physical education convention in Chicago. Ellen said, "How would you like to give clinics for the NGF?" Lorraine asked her what the NGF was and Ellen answered, "You'll just need to come and find out." That was so like Ellen.

It was our job to teach coaches at schools how to teach golf to get more people playing the game. That helped sell equipment which was the purpose of it all. We received a salary from the manufacturers for bringing people to the game and for increasing their sales. I was still on the Golfcraft Staff, but because I was representing all the manufacturers, I couldn't use my staff clubs. Golfcraft made me a special set of clubs without their name stamped on them that I could use when giving clinics.

Ellen and I conducted the first NGF Consultant Seminar at Bowling Green State University in 1967. We invited 11 to attend. The following year the seminar was held at the University of North Carolina, Greensboro. The NGF had received numerous requests from schools across the nation, so we needed to expand our consultant program. By 1970, we had 60 NGF Area Consultants.

Soon after I went to work for the NGF, a team of us compiled all their teaching material. We put together the *Golf Teaching Kit* which was a complete guide for teachers and coaches. It included: "Golf Instructor's Guide" by Ellen, Lorraine, and myself; the "Golf Coach's Guide" by Mary Dagraedt, Anne Casey Johnstone, Mary Beth Nienhaus, and Lorraine; the "Planning and Conducting Competitive Golf Events" by Mary and myself; the "Planning and Conducting Junior Golf Programs" by Ellen; the "Easy Way to Learn

1966. Western Educational Director for the
National Golf Foundation.

Golf Rules" by the NGF; and finally the "Visual Aids for Golf Instruction" which Lorraine put together from some existing material.
We produced a film called "Courtesy on the Course" that Ellen, Lorraine, and I worked on. The LPGA used these guides until the late
1980s.

By the time I started working with the NGF, I was back living in the Palms Springs area. In the winter, I had to fly to the NGF office in Chicago to work, which I hated. Ever since I was young, I've never liked to be indoors. In California, I could be outdoors while the Midwest was dealing with all the snow. I would fly to Chicago, stay at the Bismarck Hotel, and walk across the bridge to the NGF office in the Merchandise Mart.

I'd stay four or five days working on the scheduling of future seminars, clinics, and workshops. We planned a three-year calendar covering the entire country from coast to coast. A BIG thank you to Ellen who helped us get started with the nightmare of scheduling. I was never good at fitting everything together. Ellen wrote out a sample for us to follow; a three-year time sequence for our future workshops, schools, appearances, etc.

High school and college teachers could write to the NGF and ask for help. Then the NGF would send Lorraine or me to show them how to teach students and organize a program. It was our job to promote the game of golf. This wasn't only at the college level. I also went to individual high schools and high school physical education conventions. Teachers would purchase our teaching kit and visual aids. It gave them very valuable information to help them teach golf to their students.

One of the most challenging clinics I ever taught was with Lorraine at Michigan State University. We had a hundred students show up for the class. We split them into two gyms. Lorraine start-

1970s. National Golf Foundation Clinic at California State University, Fullerton for Physical Education teachers.

ed in one and I in the other. Then we crisscrossed back and forth between the two gyms. The University had even sent the players of their football team to be taught — why, I'll never know. Most of these big, muscle-bound young men weren't very flexible, but we figured out a way to help them. We survived the few days of teaching and learned a lot ourselves. A good teacher never stops learning.

On one trip, I was to give a clinic at the University of Connecticut. They picked me up at the airport in a Volkswagen. I had a golf bag with my own set of clubs, another golf bag, a couple of large duffle bags full of teaching aids, and a suitcase with my clothes. It would be extremely expensive flying with all that baggage today. It took the transportation crew three trips to get me and all my bags to where I was staying. We always carried a lot of stuff with us to use in the clinics we taught all around the country. I had brought all sorts of materials with me so that those attending the seminar could make teaching aids. I left a lot lighter than I arrived, and they all took home aids they could use to teach their students.

Lorraine and I held the first of 12 NGF National Golf Seminars in 1970 at Pine Needles Resort owned by former LPGA Tour player Peggy Kirk Bell and her husband, Warren. Pine Needles is also where Ellen, Lorraine, and I had shot the film, "Courtesy on the Course."

Warren was a former professional basketball player and went by the nickname "Bullet." After his death in 1984, Peggy ran the resort with her children. I was so sad when Peggy's son called to let me know that his mother had died — this was in November of 2016.

Starting in 1970, we held two national seminars a year, one in the East and one in the West. Here we taught the area consultants how to teach our methodology so we could be consistent. They were responsible for taking care of their regions, so Lorraine and I didn't have to run all over. Ellen had been at the forefront, and that's how we paid forward what she had started.

We invited all the nation's top teachers to come and present at these NGF National Seminars. We also had the best college coaches share their coaching techniques and what they thought were the keys to their success.

Most everyone helped out. We were blessed to have some

1970s. National Golf Foundation Clinic, Phoenix, Arizona.

of the finest teachers in the country donate their time and talent to help promote the game of golf. I hate to list the instructors because I'm sure I'll leave some out, but here are some of the many who I do remember: Dr. Gary Wiren, Jim Flick, Bob Toski, Bill Strausbaugh, Bert Yancey, Paul Bertholy, Manuel de la Torre, Jim Bailey, Conrad Rehling, Rod Myers, Dick Gordin, Bruce Fossum, Opal Hill, Patty Berg, Marilynn Smith, Peggy Kirk Bell, Ellen Griffin, Joanne Winter, Carol Johnson, Mary Dagraedt, DeDe Owens, Mary Beth Nienhaus, Barbara Smith, Goldie Bateson, Marge Burns, Ann Casey Johnstone, and Carrie Russell. I'm sure that I've forgotten a few, and for that I'm sorry, but this is quite a list of "Who's Who" in golf education.

Most of the attendees were professors. The pros talked about how the swing worked, and then the kinesiology professors would argue that the human body can't perform the way they said. They would argue back and forth on topics like: "An object cannot be released without a right angle." Each side walked away with a lot of valuable information.

One of our panel members from the PGA, Bill Strausbaugh, would say there was no difference teaching a man or a woman. I jumped up and said, "There certainly was!" I got a basketball protective bra, put it on him, and told him to swing the way he had just said.

"Oh, I can't do that," he said.

And I said, "You're right. You can't!"

It was quite enlightening and entertaining, to say the least.

Although most of my work was in the West, I had made friends in Vermont when I was the head pro at Sugarbush Golf Course. If I wanted to visit them and had a week off from my real job, teaching at Indian Wells Country Club, I would give a clinic at the Elks Club in Montpelier and charge the NGF for my trip. I would teach a five-day clinic. People could attend as many of the days as they wanted, and it cost them just one dollar per day. One dollar!

Montpelier is the state capital of Vermont where several big insurance companies were located. They employed lots of women so I would hold a morning session, an afternoon session, and one at 5:30 pm. Those who worked could come to the evening class, while people who routinely played golf during the day could come in the

*1967. Shirley teaching a National Golf Foundation Clinic,
at the Elks Club in Montpelier, Vermont.*

morning or afternoon. That geographic area basically got free golf instruction, and it served to promote the game of golf for the Golf Foundation. It was also a way for me to spend time with my East-Coast friends.

I remember a five-day seminar I taught at the University of

137

Northern Colorado in Greeley. The university had added golf instruction to their summer, graduate-course curriculum. Teachers came from all over the world for summer school, and this was just one of the subjects they were taking. Unbeknownst to me, they had signed up 100 people.

Dr. Betsy Clark was teaching in Denver at the time. I flew into Denver, and she offered to drive me to Greeley. When we got to Greeley, I saw the list of people who had signed up for the class. I told Betsy, "You can't go home. I can't do this alone! I can't teach 100 people!" So she offered to stay and help me the entire week. We divided the class into two groups and then divided it again. Some came in the morning, and some came in the afternoon. You can't teach over 25 people at a time in a group and do a good job. We had to keep changing the format. Some lessons were indoors, some outside on the campus, and some were at the local golf facility.

It could have been a nightmare, but thanks to Betsy's help it turned out fine. There was a special bond in the early days of the LPGA — everyone helped everyone else. We might have been few in numbers, but we pitched in, worked together, and helped whenever needed.

At the end of the week, we drove up to Cheyenne, Wyoming, for the Frontier Days. They had a big rodeo and even had a bull named "Sheryl." I figured that was close enough to my name, "Shirley," so I rooted for it.

It was pouring rain as we drove back to Denver. I looked over

1960s. National Golf Foundation Clinic in the snow, Amarillo, Texas.

and saw a funnel cloud off in the distance. It wasn't coming toward us, but it was raining and hailing like crazy. We turned on the radio, and there were tornado warnings right where we were driving! We knew we shouldn't be on the highway, but by that time we were three-fourths of the way to Denver, so we didn't stop. Greeley and Cheyenne were quite an adventure and all because of teaching golf.

After Ellen retired from working for the NGF, and from teaching at the university, it wasn't long before she was bored. Her brother, Dr. Charles, was a country doctor in Dyersville, Iowa, but he owned a farm in Randleman, North Carolina, just outside of Greensboro. Ellen asked her brother if she could use his land to open up a teaching facility. She built the entire facility and even mowed the grass herself. She created a nice little teaching area and called it "The Farm."

If it was raining, students could stand in the barn and hit balls out onto the field. She took videos of their swings. They could come in, sit down by a little fire, watch the video, and talk about their swings. She also held a courtesy session once a week for all her students. On a certain day, she would be there to help them at no charge. Ellen was simply an amazing person!

Later, Charles fixed up the old farmhouse, which was on the property, for Ellen to live in. During one of my visits, I set up a little club repair area on the porch so she could make some extra money to supplement her teaching. She could sell grips to her students, and I taught her how to regrip clubs.

Ellen had lots of wildlife on The Farm. One of the cardinals she called "Cardinal Cushing" after the Archbishop of Boston. There was a peahen named Carol and a peacock named Mann after one of her students. There were three ducks — Birdie, Bogey, and Par. Birdie died, but soon there was another Birdie. Tom was a fitting name for the turkey. Tom used to stand behind the golfers as they practiced on The Farm golf range. Mock, the mockingbird, had a morning ritual of attacking the cats. Ellen named a cow after herself and another one she called Babe. Her dogs and cats also had fun names like April, Snowball, Green Eyes, and Saddle Shoes. Ellen just named them all.

Ellen's brother carved a seat out of a cedar stump and named it for me after I was a guest speaker at The Farm. It was called "Shirley's Cedar Seater."

Ellen's farm had a lake on it . . . well, it was more like a pond. On one of my visits, I met her nephew, Charlie. Charlie's dad was Ellen's brother, Dr. Charles. Charlie talked about going frogging, and I said I'd go with him. We grabbed a flashlight and a stick with a prong on it. Then we hopped into this metal boat. Charlie and I paddled to the other side of the pond, got out of the boat, and gigged for frogs. We caught about six frogs and headed back to the farmhouse to cook them. When we moored the boat, I stood up, and the round-bottomed boat flipped over! The flashlight flew into the pond, the frogs went back into the pond, and I fell in the pond. I had a girdle on and was covered from head to toe in Georgia clay. We walked back to the farmhouse, and Dr. Charles was waiting there with a camera. He took pictures of me dripping wet, covered in mud. It was the funniest thing. So yes, I've been frogging once but didn't get to eat any of them since we dumped them back into the pond.

Phyllis Otto was a great amateur golfer. She won the Women's National Collegiate Golf Championship in 1946 beating Dorothy Germain in the final match. This was the year before I won it. I played against both Phyllis and Dot in collegiate events — Dorothy went by "Dot," not Dorothy. Phyllis later married Dot's brother, so I guess there weren't any hard feelings from all their years competing against each other. They were always very close, the best of friends, and neither of them ever turned pro.

Dot was also a wonderful amateur golfer. She's in the USGA

history book as the winner of both the U.S. Women's Amateur and the U.S. Women's Senior Amateur. Dot's nickname was "Flower" because she wore flower dresses. Most of us wore plain culottes.

Phyllis had a daughter, and she named her Dorothy after her sister-in-law. I met this younger "Dot" at Ellen's farm. Unlike her mother and aunt, Dot turned pro and later was president of the LPGA Tour. She worked at The Farm and went to college at Greensboro which had its own 9-hole golf course on campus.

UNC-Greensboro was also where DeDe Owens got her master's degree. DeDe later earned her doctorate at the University of Virginia. She played the Tour briefly and then taught golf. DeDe was giving a lesson at Cog Hill Country Club in Chicago when she suffered a heart attack. She died a few days later. It was a shock because she was so young, only 53 years old. DeDe was a great teacher. She and I are the only two who have received the LPGA Teacher of the Year Award twice.

Carol Mann also attended Ellen's alma mater in Greensboro. Once when I was visiting Ellen, she said, "See that lady coming up the hill? She's going to be a great player." Carol stood over six feet tall – you couldn't miss her. Carol went on to win 38 tournaments, including two majors, and is in the World Golf Hall of Fame. So, as you can see, history proved Ellen right.

Aside from the NGF, the LPGA held golf schools from 1960 to 1966. We invited female coaches and physical education teachers to come and learn how to teach all levels of the game and how to

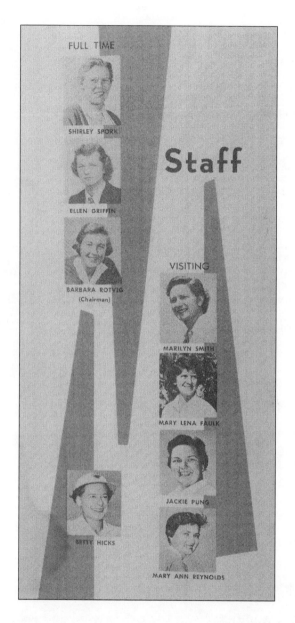

1960s. The staff of the LPGA National Golf Schools
was a group of renowned women golfers.

instruct both men and woman students. At the end of the week, they gave three lessons and took a written test. Two of the lessons could be to people who already played the game, while the third one might be to someone who had never touched a golf club. We would observe their teaching and then pass or fail them. If they passed, they were given a certificate saying they had passed both the written and practical exams. Then they could apply to become a member of the LPGA Teaching Division.

All we wanted was standardization. We wanted instructors to teach a method. It didn't have to be our personal method. It just had to be a way of hitting the ball until it ended up in the cup. Any teacher can just get out there and say, "Ok, here we are. What would you like to work on?" But we wanted them to show their students how to move the ball from tee to green.

We structured it and standardized the method. For instance, when teaching a group, the right-handed players hit from a certain place in the line and the left-handed in another. This was primarily for safety. If it was a big group, you placed them in lines, and they rotated. They weren't all hitting at the same time. These were all things instructors needed to know.

After I accepted a full-time position with the NGF Education Division in 1966, the LPGA Executive Board (which consisted of Tour players) said that me remaining as the chairperson of the LPGA Teaching Division would be a conflict of interest, so I was asked to resign. Penny Zavichas was appointed chairperson, and unfortunately, the LPGA National Golf Schools came to an end.

In 1975 Mary Dagraedt took over as the national chairperson of the teaching committee. She believed that it would be easier and more effective to manage the teaching division if we divided the U.S. into sections. Mary patterned it after the model used by the American Association for Health, Physical Education, and Recreation. There would be five sections: Northeast, Southeast, Midwest, Central, and Western. Golf has grown on such a global scale that in 2015 we added our sixth section — the International Section.

The vote to form into sections finally passed the membership in 1975, and we in the West were ready. It took the rest of the country time to get organized, but we got right on it. I scheduled a seminar at Indian Wells Country Club where I was teaching. Pat Lange co-chaired the workshop with me, and Joanne Winter helped us teach. I called all the ladies who I thought might want to join our section to attend this workshop so we could tell them all about the LPGA Teaching Division. Twenty ladies showed up, and almost everyone joined our western section. That's how we got started. I was voted president, and we were off and running. Now we have over 1,700 members in the LPGA Teaching and Club Professional Division.

In 1983 we held our first LPGA Teaching Division National Championship. It was held at Placid Lakes Golf Club in Lake Placid, Florida. It gave our teaching members a chance to showcase their playing skills and at first was held every other year. In 1993 it became a yearly event, and now the top eight finishers earn exemptions to compete in the KPMG Women's PGA Championship.

We also hold the LPGA Teaching & Club Professional Team Championship which is a yearly, two-person team event that started in 1991.

I remember one of the tournaments held in Naples, Florida. There were wild boar on the course. We were not to go into the rough on certain holes because they would attack. We were allowed a free drop back on the fairway.

We also were told not to feed the alligators that gathered near the clubhouse, but I remember watching the chef feed them raw meat. I didn't find this very amusing since it was so dangerous. It just goes to show you all the hazards which golfers face on the course.

When Shirley Spork and I first met at the Women's National Collegiate Golf Championship in 1948, we had no idea that we would be co-founders of the LPGA Tour and lifelong friends.

The first year of the Tour we traveled from tournament to tournament in my green Dodge Coronet. When Shirley drove, she put a piece of tape over the speedometer so I couldn't see if we were breaking my father's rule of not exceeding the speed limit. When driving through small towns, we often stopped and played catch. A baseball and our gloves were always in the trunk. We never left home without them.

Once I attended a Catholic Mass with Shirley and another week she went with me to a Congregational Church in Connecticut. She said, "Oh my, I'm going to have to go to confession." I asked her how she liked going to church with me. She said, "It all depends if you want to go to heaven in a Ford or in a Cadillac."

For over 60 years Shirley has been an exceptional golf instructor. She tried to start a teaching division for three years, but the players voted it down. That was until 1959 when I was LPGA President. Shirley, Barbara Rotvig, Betty Hicks, and I worked to get the player's approval and it passed by one vote. That single vote has blossomed into an organization of more than 1,700 Teaching and Club Professionals.

When checking out my golf swing, Shirley always stressed TEMPO. I wrote the word "TEMPO" on a piece of paper and taped it to the mirror in my motel room. It served as a reminder to make a smooth backswing.

Golf is a game of a lifetime. At age 85, Shirley hit a hybrid 123 yards for a hole-in-one while playing the Marilynn Smith LPGA Celebrity Pro-Am in Goodyear, Arizona. She always did know how to steal the show.

No one could have a better friend than Shirley Spork. Throughout the years I have known Shirley, she has always been willing to help people. She has a big heart and there isn't anything she wouldn't do for anybody.

God bless you, Shirley.

Marilynn Smith

LPGA Tour - Founding Member

LPGA Teaching & Club Professional - Founding Member

World Golf Hall of Fame

HOLE # 7

Founding Members of the LPGA Tour

The early Tour showed a slow but steady growth in the 1950s. There certainly were some hurdles to overcome, like Babe's untimely death in 1956. A few names were added to the roster each year throughout the '50s, but with attrition, the weekly field remained small. By 1960, approximately 65 women had left the amateur ranks and called themselves LPGA Professionals. Not exactly an explosion over a 10-year span.

Shirley played the LPGA Tour sporadically throughout the 1950s splitting her time between playing and teaching. As one of the 13 Founding Members, she has some unique insight and fun memories of times spent with her contemporaries.

Helen Hicks

I never met Helen Hicks, who was one of our founding members. Fred Corcoran was our tour director, and his lawyer's office was in New York. When the papers were drawn up for the LPGA Tour, the law stated that at least one of the signatures needed to come from a New York resident. Helen signed the charter because she happened to live on Long Island.

Helen had a remarkable amateur career winning several major tournaments in the 1930s. She was also a member of the first Curtis Cup Team. The Curtis Cup is the Solheim Cup of the women's amateur golf world. The Curtis Cup, however, is the United States versus Great Britain and Ireland whereas the Solheim Cup is the United States versus Europe. The first Curtis Cup was held in 1932 at the Wentworth Club in England, and the American team won.

Helen was one of the first, if not **the** first, woman to turn pro. This was way back in 1934 when she was only 23 years old. Helen went to work for Wilson Sporting Goods and also wrote articles for the *American Golfer Magazine* which was edited by the legendary sportswriter Grantland Rice.

In Helen's day, women amateurs didn't have much respect for women turning pro, so she called herself a "businesswoman golfer." She invented the idea of traveling all over the country to give clinics. She was a great ambassador and saleswoman for Wilson. Opal Hill joined Helen a few years later (1938) also giving clinics for Wilson. These two women opened the door for Helen Dettweiler, who joined the Wilson Staff in 1939 and then Patty Berg in 1940. Patty was best known for her clinics, but she owes some of her success to the three women who went before her and blazed the trail.

Opal Hill

Opal Hill was from Kansas City, Missouri and another one of

our 13 founders. She was part Native American Indian. She was already 58 years old when we started the LPGA Tour in 1950 but had a remarkable amateur career. She was Helen Hicks' contemporary. They competed throughout the 1930s and were teammates on the first Curtis Cup Team in 1932.

Opal only played in a handful of LPGA tournaments. I remember playing with her at the 1951 U.S. Women's Open in Atlanta, Georgia.

Several years later, Opal was invited to play in a National Golf Foundation (NGF) tournament. It was a 9-hole scramble, and she was on my team. Opal had a putter with a little loft on it. When she putted, the ball hopped up into the air the first foot-and-a-half or so. Then it landed back on the green and rolled right into the cup. It was something unusual to see. Opal had nine one-putts and our team won! What an experience to watch Opal's putting style that day; it's something I'll never forget.

When I was the chairperson of the LPGA Teaching Division, Opal sent me a letter. She wanted help on how to approach and present herself to the management of the golf courses in her area. She was older by then and was having trouble being recognized as a teacher. She wanted to become established so she could earn a living wage. In those days, it wasn't easy to get a teaching job and get paid. She was struggling financially at the time, and there was no guarantee of making a living as a teacher. Opal wanted to teach, and the golf facilities wanted a percent of her lesson money, so she wrote to ask my advice. I suggested that she negotiate — give something to receive something.

Babe Didrikson Zaharias

I won't say much about Babe here since I've already shared several stories about her. However, I will say that if Yankee Stadium is the house that Babe (Ruth) built, the LPGA is the Tour that Babe (Didrikson Zaharias) built!

You can't have a tour without all the supporting players, but you need to have a star or two — someone to land the sponsors and bring the public out to watch. That was Babe, and she knew it! She would walk into the locker room and say, "The Babe is here. Who's going to be second?" Some of the other golfers didn't appreciate her brashness, but I believe everyone knew that the Tour needed her.

Babe was a "star" and very comfortable playing that role. She was also a "ham," very vocal and playful with the gallery, and they loved that. It was quite a blow to the Tour when Babe died in 1956. Kudos to the veterans and newcomer Mickey Wright on keeping the LPGA Tour alive.

Helen Dettweiler

Founding member, Helen Dettweiler, accomplished so much in her life. She grew up in the Washington, D.C. area and graduated from Trinity College now known as Trinity Washington University. It was one of the nation's first Roman Catholic women's colleges. She also took law classes at night. Helen graduated but didn't bother to take the Bar Exam because there wasn't much of a market for women lawyers in the 1930s.

Helen played amateur tournaments and became close friends with Clark Griffith who owned part of the Washington Senators. In 1938, he hired Helen to do the play-by-play on national radio. She was the first woman to be an announcer for a men's professional baseball team.

In 1939, Helen gave up her amateur status and joined the Wilson Sporting Goods team giving clinics with Helen Hicks and Opal Hill.

World War II came along, and she joined the WASPs — Women Airforce Service Pilots. Helen ferried planes, including the B-17 bomber, known as the "Flying Fortress." She loved that plane and always said, "I didn't fly the B-17, it flew itself."

Helen later headed up the cryptology department in Washington, D.C. She commanded a staff of women who were sent around the nation to set up code-breaking operations. She was so smart, brilliant actually.

After the war, she taught at O'Donnell Golf Club. She was the very first lady pro in the Palms Springs area.

Jacqueline "Jackie" Cochran was an aviation pioneer and a good friend of Amelia Earhart. After Amelia's disappearance in 1937, Jackie became the premier female aviator in the country. She was the driving force in forming the WASPs, which is where she and Helen met.

Jackie and her husband, Floyd Odlum, owned a large ranch near Indio, California. Helen helped Jackie with her golf game and writing her memoirs. At one point, Floyd asked Jackie why she drove all the way to Palm Springs to golf when they had so much land? They asked Helen to design, build, and be the head pro of a 9-hole course on their ranch. Today it's a 27-hole course called Indian Palms Country Club.

After the course was built, Helen told the foreman to buy a particular seed for the greens which cost ten times more than fairway seed. The grass was planted, started to grow, and she went out to take a look. She said, "There's something wrong here. These greens are the same as the fairways!"

"Yes," the foreman said, "that other seed was too expensive, so I didn't buy it."

Helen told him, "You have to use the more expensive seed for the greens!" She had them rip out the grass and replant all the greens.

President Dwight D. Eisenhower was a close personal friend of Floyd and Jackie and often vacationed in the Palm Springs area. Whenever he was in town, he had a standing 8:30 lesson with Helen before heading out for his morning round of golf.

Helen ran her friend's course for a few years and then in 1952 became the first female golf pro at Thunderbird Country Club in Rancho Mirage. Thunderbird was the first 18-hole course in the Coachella Valley and had just opened the year before.

Have you ever wondered about motorized golf carts used on golf courses all over the world? Well, that innovation was started at Thunderbird Country Club while Helen was working there.

After leaving Thunderbird, she taught for a short time at El Dorado Country Club. Helen worked with some very good golfers, including Beverly Hanson who was from North Dakota and later played the Tour.

Helen had the first ladies' sportswear shop in the area. Her store was on El Paseo, the Rodeo Drive of Palm Springs. She and her brother, who worked for the FBI, designed and had the store built. They owned that whole corner of El Paseo and San Luis Rey Avenue. Helen's shop was at street level, and Billy's FBI office was upstairs.

Helen was an associate and a good friend of mine. We often played Tour events together, which was only in the summer when we weren't teaching. Helen was an amazing teacher and received the first LPGA Teacher of the Year Award in 1958. My dear friend died in 1990 which was a great loss for me and the entire golfing world here in the Palm Springs area.

Patty Berg

Patty Berg always said that she was nine holes ahead of me. She was born in 1918, and I was born in 1927. We were built alike, and since we both had red hair, we looked alike . . . at least from a distance. When I played in George S. May's Tam O'Shanter tournament outside of Chicago, there were times that the gallery thought

1960. Shirley's number from the Tam O'Shanter
All-American Golf Tournament.

I was Patty and would follow me. We wore numbers pinned on our backs. Once the spectators looked up the number in their program and saw I wasn't Patty, they'd disappear!

Patty probably gave more clinics than any of us in the U.S., somewhere around 10,000. She had gone to the Carnegie School to learn how to communicate effectively. Her program was scripted and always the same, which was the opposite of me. Every talk I gave was different. I let it fly off the top of my head . . . just let it go.

Patty was an entertainer, a great player, and took lots of golf lessons throughout her life. She always had a coach, but the main influence in her game was Les Bolstad who coached the University of Minnesota golf team for 30 years.

156

*Early 1950's. Patty Berg and Shirley checking the
swing weight of a club at the Wilson factory.*

Patty signed with the Wilson Sporting Goods Company in 1940 and was an extremely dedicated member of their staff during her entire golf career. With Patty, it was always Wilson, Wilson, Wilson! She would only autograph Wilson golf balls! In fact, at her funeral in 2006, each honorary LPGA pallbearer tossed a Wilson golf ball into the grave as they lowered Patty's casket.

An interesting note about Wilson Sporting Goods is its history with a meat-packing plant in Chicago. In 1913, the company that owned the packing plant founded the Ashland Manufacturing Company to use the by-products from its slaughterhouse. Thomas

Wilson was named the president of Ashland in 1915 and the following year he broke away and started his own company. He named it Wilson Sporting Goods. He used his contacts in the meat-packing industry to buy hides. That's where he got the leather to make golf bags. Wilson became the biggest name in golf bags.

Patty also endorsed Peter Pan Peanut Butter. We used to kid her about it all the time — "Here comes Peter Pan Peanut Butter Patty." It was hard to say. A real tongue twister.

Patty had the rookies clean her shoes at the tournaments. Just before she left the course for the day, she'd place her shoes outside her locker. The rookies knew the drill and Patty always wore clean shoes.

She was a good friend who would do anything for you. Patty had a great sense of humor, got along well with the other players and was one of the stars of the early LPGA Tour.

Louise Suggs

Louise Suggs was a very quiet, reserved, cooperative, friendly person. She had a beautiful golf swing. Bob Hope nicknamed her "Miss Sluggs," because she hit the ball so far, but I called her "Suggsy."

She was from Georgia — a Georgia Peach. Her father, Johnny, was a left-handed pitcher for the Atlanta Crackers baseball club. The team, which was owned by his future father-in-law, was part of the Yankees farm system. During one of the Crackers games, the Spalding Company offered to give a set of clubs to any pitcher who hit a home run. Johnny hit a home run, got a set of clubs, and later said that's why he took up golf.

After he had married the boss's daughter, Johnny quit pitching to run the ballpark concession stands. On the night Louise was born, (September 7, 1923) the ballpark burned down. Shortly after that, Johnny and his family moved 15 miles down the road to Lithia Springs where he managed a 9-hole golf course. It was there that Louise learned to play golf. She would follow her father around their golf course with a cut-down, hickory-shafted club from Spalding.

Years later, in 1948, Johnny was hired as the head golf pro of a brand-new 9-hole course 35 miles away in Carrollton, Georgia. It was named Sunset Hills Country Club, and we had a LPGA Tour stop there in the 1950s. The caddies were young boys and they all had baseball gloves. When we would practice, they would snag our shots like they were fielding fly balls.

When you think of Georgia, you think of peaches, but few people know that Georgia was and still is pimento country. Back in the 1930s, several small towns including Carrollton claimed that they were the pimento capital of the world. I always think of this when I eat the olives that have been marinating in my evening vodka. That's also probably why pimento cheese is so popular in the South.

As is typical in the South, Carrollton had a small, quaint downtown. All the little businesses were arranged around the town square. One year when I went to play, the owner of the local pharmacy came out to watch the tournament. After I finished my round, he said his wife was serving birds for dinner and asked if I'd ever had them. I thought, "I wonder what he's talking about?"

He told me, "I'll come fetch ya and tote ya here."

I said, "Yeah, ok — you can pick me up and bring me back."

I went over to his home for dinner and learned that the birds he was talking about were quail . . . ones he had shot earlier in the day. His wife brought out this big platter, piled high with these very small birds. I had never eaten quail before and spent the night picking buckshot out of my dinner trying not to chip a tooth.

At the gas station in Carrollton, they washed your windows, which was not unusual for the time. But first, they'd take a corncob and scratch your windows to get the bugs off. Then they'd dunk the corncob in a bucket of water, wash the window and dry it with a rag. I'd never seen that before.

When Louise graduated from high school, she went to work as a clerk for Gulf Oil. She stayed with them until she turned pro in 1948. Gulf Oil helped sponsor her Tour dreams and supplied her with a new Cadillac every year. While on the Tour she would let me drive her car, one of over 40 Cadillacs she owned in her lifetime.

For years, Louise lived with her poodle named Dammit on the adjoining property of the World Golf Hall of Fame near St. Augustine, Florida. The LPGA Hall of Fame is housed there, too. It merged with the World Golf Hall of Fame when it moved from Augusta, Georgia, in 1998. Louise was one of the first women to be inducted into the LPGA and World Golf Hall of Fame. She, Babe, Patty, and Betty Jameson were all inducted in 1951. Louise won 61 times on the Tour which is fourth all-time. Only Kathy Whitworth, Mickey Wright, and Annika Sorenstam have more Tour victories than Louise. Patty Berg is fifth with 60 wins.

After she had retired from the Tour, Louise taught for years at Sea Island Resort in Georgia. She would go there in the winter.

We were very good friends, and I was so sad when she passed away in August of 2015 at the age of 91. She is sorely missed by everyone.

Alice and Marlene Bauer

Then there were the Bauer sisters: Alice and Marlene. Alice was my age and Marlene is seven years younger. Marlene was only 16 when she joined the Tour in 1950 and finished high school by mail.

The Bauer family came from Eureka, South Dakota. They moved to Long Beach, California, where their father managed a driving range. He was also their coach. Papa Bauer would lay a bed sheet out on the ground and have Alice and Marlene practice landing balls on it from various distances. On the Tour, there was always a standing bet among the players on how many chips the sisters would hole out during their round. They both had very good short games.

Their father also invented a teaching aid. While the girls were practicing, if he detected an error in their backswing, he could pull this string and knock the ball off the tee so they couldn't hit it. Both the girls had really long backswings that dipped way beyond parallel at the top.

When we were all still amateurs, I played with the Bauer sisters in the Tam O'Shanter tournament. I remember walking into the locker room after my round and saw Alice sitting there crying, trying to catch her breath. I thought, "Oh my God, somebody died," and I asked Alice, "what's the matter?"

"Today my father said if I shot 76 or better I could have five dollars to buy some new shoes, and I shot 77!"

I felt sorry for Alice. That seemed like a lot of added pressure to me. Papa Bauer was from the old country; a German colony in Odessa, Russia. He was tough on his daughters.

The United States Golf Association (USGA) had questioned the sisters' amateur standing because Papa Bauer was collecting money for their clinics. It could have caused a scene at the 1950 Women's National Amateur Championship, but before the tournament, Alice and Marlene turned pro. Their first appearance as pros — or "Proettes" as the media called us — was at the 1950 Pebble Beach Weathervane the last week of April. I turned pro the following week at the Weathervane in Chicago.

Alice's name was Alice Bauer Hagge Hovey, and Marlene is Marlene Bauer Hagge Vossler. Both girls were married to Robert Hagge, but not at the same time of course. Not too long after Alice and Robert divorced, Marlene and Robert got married. Alice and Robert had a daughter. Her name is Heidi Hagge Hovey Gussa.

Marlene is Heidi's aunt and stepmother. Very unusual.

Marlene later married Ernie Vossler who was well known in the Palm Springs area. He was a golf course architect and chairman of Landmark Golf which built golf communities in the Coachella Valley as well as throughout the country.

Alice passed away in 2002. Marlene still lives near me in the Palm Springs area.

Bettye Mims Danoff

Betty Mims was also a founding member of the LPGA Tour. She decided to add an "e" to her name as a teenager which made it Bettye. Bettye started playing golf at the age of six. Her family owned a 9-hole golf course and driving range in Grand Prairie, Texas, now called the Sunset Golf Club. I believe it is still run by the family. That is where Babe Zaharias sharpened her golf game.

Bettye's claim to fame was that she beat Babe in the 1947 Texas Women's Open in Fort Worth. This ended Babe's 17-tournament winning streak. Bettye was small, a little over five foot and 106 pounds. The girls on the Tour nicknamed her "Mighty Mite" because she hit the ball so long off the tee.

In 1949, Bettye married Dr. Clyde Walter Danoff. That's why you'll find her name in the record books as Bettye Danoff.

I remember her bringing her three daughters on the Tour with her. She was the first mother to do so. Many times it was hard for Bettye to find someone to watch the girls while she was competing.

Her husband died in 1961 at a young age. Bettye was only 38 years old when she became a widow. She was part of our cross-country caravan before her husband died, but even then, she played a limited schedule — mostly the tournaments in Texas and Oklahoma. Soon after he died, Bettye retired from the Tour to raise her daughters.

Glenda Kay is the oldest daughter. She's from Bettye's first marriage which was brief. In 1960, Glenda Kay had a baby, making "Mighty Mite" the first and only grandmother playing on the LPGA Tour. Bettye was only 36 when she became a grandmother.

During the Swing Parade Clinics that we put on before the tournaments, Patty Berg would introduce Bettye as "Grandma." Bettye would come out dressed up in all these old clothes. She sprayed her hair gray and wore these little gold-rimmed glasses that sat on the tip of her nose. She'd limp out with a walking stick and then whack the ball out of sight.

I recently saw one of Bettye's daughters at the Founders Cup Tournament in Phoenix, Arizona, where Bettye was being honored. It was fun listening to the stories of her adventures traveling with her mother on the LPGA Tour as a little girl.

Bettye passed away in December 2011 in McKinney, Texas.

Sally Sessions

Sally Sessions and I were both from Michigan. Sally was actually a great amateur tennis player and won the state title when she was only 16 years old. Not long after that, she took up golf. Sally took lessons from Lee Kosten who was the professional at Muskegon Country Club and soon became the top golfer in the area. Not only was she a great athlete, she also was an accomplished musician and wrote operas.

Sally won both the Muskegon City Amateur Tennis and Amateur Golf Championships in 1942, which was quite a remarkable feat since both tournaments were held on the same day! She was Michigan State Amateur Champion in 1946, three years before I won it in 1949. Since we were both from Michigan, we competed against one another in amateur tournaments over the years.

The following year, at the 1947 U.S. Women's Open at the Starmount Forest Country Club in Greensboro, North Carolina, Sally and Polly Riley finished tied for second behind Betty Jameson. Betty was a pro and Sally and Polly both played as amateurs at the Open that year. They held a sudden-death playoff and Sally sunk a birdie putt on the first hole to beat Polly for low amateur.

Sally hosted a little tournament in her hometown of Muskegon. I remember playing in it. It was on a 9-hole golf course and the year I played, Patty Berg won. That was the summer of 1947, during the Women's Professional Golf Association (WPGA) years — before the LPGA Tour was formed.

In the fall of 1947, Sally won the Mexican National Amateur Golf Championship. Soon after, she became the first woman to break men's par, shooting a 69 at the famed Pinehurst Country Club in North Carolina.

Early in 1948, Sally turned pro joining the Wilson Sporting Goods staff. She finished fifth at the 1949 Tam O'Shanter All-American, which was her best finish as a pro. After that, her golf game started to slip, and none of us knew why. A short time later, Sally was diagnosed with leukemia.

Sally only played one year on the LPGA Tour. She left after the 1950 season and taught in the Detroit Public School system. Sally retired from teaching in February of 1966 and died later that year in December. At the age of 43, she was even younger than Babe.

Betty Jameson

In the early '50s, five founding members dominated the LPGA Tour: Babe Zaharias, Patty Berg, Louise Suggs, Marilynn Smith, and Betty Jameson. Betty was not only a fine golfer; she was the first "glamor girl" on the Tour. The press liked to take pictures of pretty women golfers and portrayed both Betty and the Bauer sisters (Alice and Marlene) this way. Reading old newspaper clippings is quite entertaining. "Chunky" and "freckled-faced" were adjectives used to describe Patty. Babe was "athletic." Louise was "sturdy" and "steady." Betty was "a cute blonde" and "quiet-spoken." Alice and Marlene were "slim," "trim," and "cute."

Height, weight, age, hometowns and past records were often used to describe us. A newspaper article might read something like this: "The five-foot-eight, 120-pound, trim blond from Dallas, who at 28 years old, is the reigning Women's Western Open Champion, shot a 70 today, leading the field of 12 professional golfers at 'X' Country Club." Reporting has sure changed over the years.

Betty was a free spirit and somewhat aloof. It seemed to me that she had a Jekyll-and-Hyde personality. One day you were her best friend and the next day she wouldn't say hello. She was like a windshield wiper — on, off, on, off.

As a Christian Scientist, Betty always read the *Christian Science Monitor* newspaper. She was also into modern art and really loved abstract art. When we were on the Tour and came to a town that had a museum, she would always go and check out the local talent.

Betty won the U.S. Women's Open in 1947, but will probably be most remembered for the one she lost . . . for Jackie Pung. Jackie won the 1957 Open but was disqualified. Betty had kept Jackie's scorecard and wrote the wrong number down on one of the holes. Jackie didn't check it hole by hole because the total was correct — she signed it, turned it in and was disqualified.

One year at the Tam O'Shanter Golf Course outside of Chicago, Betty had received a new set of Spalding irons that had a sheath covering the shaft. She sat there with a knife and cut it all off. She wouldn't play with them that way because she couldn't handle it visually. The artist in her nature made her very visual. It's amazing to me that she would hit them well since cutting off the covering changed the balance.

Betty always had to have her clubs with her. She would never leave her clubs at the golf course, even if they offered to store them. It didn't matter how far our motel was; she always lugged her golf bag into her room.

Betty thought it would be nice to honor the player with the lowest scoring average for the year. So in 1952, she donated a trophy and named it after one of her idols, the legendary Glenna Collett Vare. Glenna had grown up in Rhode Island and was probably one of the greatest amateurs to ever play the game. Patty Berg won the first trophy in 1953. Kathy Whitworth has won the most with seven. Pros on the LPGA Tour today still vie for that coveted trophy which Betty started over six decades ago.

Betty was one of four inaugural members of the Hall of Fame of Women's Golf. She, along with Babe, Patty, and Louise, was voted in when the Hall was established by the LPGA in 1951. It was later renamed the LPGA Tour Hall of Fame and then in 1998 merged with the PGA. Now it's known as The World Golf Hall of Fame which is located in St. Augustine, Florida.

Marilynn Smith

Marilynn Smith is probably my longest-living friend. We met at the 1948 Women's National Collegiate Golf Championship held at Ohio State University. We traveled together in the early days of the Tour and have remained close friends our entire lives.

1952. Shirley and Marilynn Smith, two great LPGA friends who each wanted to win the Weathervane Women's Open Championship.

Marilynn was known as "Miss Personality" on the Tour. Some people thought she was putting on an act, because she was so nice to everybody. But, that's honestly who Marilynn is and has always been. She has always been very outgoing and extremely generous. We have been friends for almost 70 years, so I should know. I remember times when the caddies would ask her for a little money to tide them over until the next tournament and Marilynn never turned anyone down.

Marilynn was interested in everybody she ever met. She had to know their name and where they were from. For example, we would pull into a gas station, and she would immediately start talking to the attendant. She would say something like; "Hi! I'm Marilynn Smith, founder of the LPGA. What's your name? Oh, it looks like you need a new pair of shoes. Here's 20 bucks." Who knows what they did with the money, but she always tried to meet people's needs.

Marilynn led lots of golf tours. She took people to places like Australia and New Zealand and gave clinics all over the world. She was a great ambassador for women's golf.

Marilynn always valued people's input. Once at the Dinah Shore Tournament she came up to me and said, "Come watch me. Come watch me! Which driver should I use? Let me hit this and see what you think."

After I had watched her hit both drivers, I put the clubs behind my back, shuffled them and held one out. "Marilynn, this is the one." I walked away, and someone else came up. She asked them the same question. Finally, it was time to tee off, and she still didn't know which driver to use.

At most of the tournament stops, Marilynn would find a local pro and take a lesson. She kept changing her swing. I told her, "Marilynn, you've got a great golf swing, just trust it! Don't fiddle with it." Marilynn had something like 23 professional wins, but I think she could have won twice as many tournaments if she could have trusted her swing. She was always tinkering with it.

I remember sitting and watching Marilynn take lessons from Tommy Armour. He would sit in a chair, under a large umbrella, and drink a gin fizz. His caddy would tee up the balls. He only had vision in one eye because of an injury from World War I. After every shot, his caddy would point left, right, or up so Tommy knew what direction the ball traveled.

Tommy never said much of anything. He didn't teach methodology. He taught his students how to think. He'd say, "What club are you from? Oh, Forest Hills Country Club. How would you play the 14th hole?" Then he'd talk about the 14th hole. "I think you should try playing that hole with your three wood or use your four iron, and aim at the center of the green, to the left of the bunker." Tommy knew all the courses like the back of his hand. He'd played them all and had a great memory.

When it came to helping a student with their stance or grip, he didn't do it — he just sat in his chair. He talked a lot. He did say one thing though that caught my attention. He said, "You get off of it, but you stay on it."

I thought, "What is he talking about? You get off it, but you stay on it." It took me awhile, but I finally figured it out. He was talking about the weight transfer. Even though you're shifting your weight to the right (your back foot), you still have pressure on your left foot (which is your target side or front foot).

Tommy had a box of spikes which were the kind roofers used on the soles of their shoes to keep from falling off the roof. Tommy had his students screw these spikes along the inside edge of their target shoe, from the instep to the toe. When they took their club back,

1950s. Marilynn and Shirley dressed to a tee.

they were supposed to dig those spikes into the ground. He wanted them to feel pressure on the spikes while actually transferring their weight to their rear foot.

When we played with some of our Tour members, we would look at their shoes and say, "Oh, you've been to see Armour." We could tell because their target shoe still had spikes in it. That was true of Betty Jameson, Mary Lena Faulk, and Jackie Pung, just to name a few. Tommy also worked with Babe and Lawson Little (whose house I stayed in the first time I played at Pebble Beach Golf Links).

The weight transfer was one thing that Tommy actually did teach, but since he was working with such good golfers, he didn't tell them how to swing the club, he just said, "Go do it." He talked a lot about the mental game and course management.

Marilynn introduced the left-hand-low putting grip. It's the grip that many of the Tour players use today. She didn't use it very long because people told her it looked strange.

Except for her pearls, Marilynn was as uncertain about her wardrobe as she was about her golf swing. "Should I wear this today? Wait, let me get the other top. Do you like this one better?" she would ask.

I'd answer, "I don't care which one you wear. Just put something on so we can get going!"

During the early days, we used to have to promote our upcoming tournaments. We were at the 1949 U.S. Women's Open Golf Championship in Landover, Maryland, and Marilynn and I volunteered to help. They sent us to a boxing match and we were seated in the front row! We were to go in the ring, be introduced, and invite the crowd to watch our golf tournament the following day. Once the fight started, blood splatted all over Marilynn and me. Marilynn was always well dressed and always wore pearls, even to the boxing match! At the end of the first match, they announced us. "Tonight we have from the ladies golf tour, Miss Shirley Spork, and Miss Marilynn Smith!" I climbed into the ring and waved, but Marilynn couldn't force herself to move. She just sat there covered in the boxers' sweat and blood.

I have this gold, signet ring. It looks a little like a high school graduation ring. On its face is the original crest of the LPGA which is two golf clubs crossed with a crown above them. It comes from a drawing that my lifelong friend, Jane Woolley, had made for the LPGA.

Some of Marilynn's Texas friends had a jeweler in Dallas make her a ring using Jane's drawing. I believe it was when she was inducted into the Texas Hall of Fame in 1994.

Jane had the same jeweler make an identical ring for me when I was inducted into the LPGA Teaching Hall of Fame in 2000. When a Tour player is inducted into the Hall of Fame, the LPGA presents them with a ring that has their birthstone in the center. They don't do that for teaching professionals, so Jane had a ring made for me. There were only two; Marilynn had one, and I had one. It meant so much to me since Jane had designed it.

LPGA logo designed and drawn by Shirley's friend, Jane Woolley. This logo is on the ring, originally owned by Marilynn Smith, that Shirley wears.

In April of 2013, all my jewelry was stolen. The ring, which had my name engraved in it, was gone. When Marilynn found out, she said, "That ring means more to you than it does to me, so you can have mine." She put her ring in the mail, and I waited and waited. I had quite a scare because I kept checking at the post office and it hadn't arrived. Finally, they found it! Someone had laid it aside; instead of putting it my box. The ring I wear now has no name in it because it was Marilynn's.

I received a Rolex watch when I was honored with the LPGA

Ellen Griffin Award in 1998. That watch and that ring are my greatest treasures, and I'm grateful to Marilynn for sharing her ring with me.

In 2006, Marilynn's contribution to the game was recognized when she was inducted into the World Golf Hall of Fame — a deserving honor for a colleague and dear friend.

Marilynn lives in Goodyear, Arizona. She is still active in golf; hosting the Marilynn Smith LPGA Charity Pro-Am each fall. 2017 marks the ninth year of Marilynn's tournament. Money raised at this event goes toward scholarships awarded to young women attending college.

I really do not remember when I first met Shirley Spork, but it seems as though I at least knew about her ever since I knew about the LPGA. My parents first introduced me to the LPGA Tour in 1959. They took me to a tournament in Alliance, Ohio. It was after that when I began to study and learn about the 13 founders who blazed the trail for those of us who were to become professional golfers and join the Tour. Shirley was always one of my dad's favorites because he liked her spunk and she also soon became one of my favorites.

Shirley's significant contribution to golf, and especially for women golfers, has been teaching the game in a way that made learning easy and enjoyable. Every time I talk to Shirley it is like going to school. I am constantly learning because she is constantly teaching.

In 2000 when the LPGA celebrated its 50th Anniversary my ladies team won the Shirley Spork Pro-Am and they have never stopped talking about it. Meeting Shirley Spork was a highlight in their golfing experience.

During the 60th year of the LPGA, we invited Shirley to be the special guest during our Clearview LPGA Pro-Am in East Canton, Ohio. It was such a treat to have one of the 13 founders come to our course.

It has been in more recent years that I have actually had the opportunity to spend more time with Shirley and I so value those moments. In 2014 Kathy Whitworth and I were honored by the LPGA with the Pioneer Award during the Founders Cup. The biggest enjoyment for me during that LPGA tournament was to be able to spend an entire week with both Shirley Spork and Marilynn Smith. Since 1967 I have been a member of the LPGA and to be able to spend time and learn from those who actually founded our organization is a gift that few people are able to experience.

My greatest friendships have come from golf and I am blessed to be able to call Shirley Spork a friend.

Dr. Renee Powell
LPGA Tour - Life Member
LPGA Teaching & Club Professional - Honorary Member
Clearview Golf Club, East Canton, Ohio - Owner
Royal and Ancient Golf Club - Honorary Member

HOLE # 8

Tour Friends

Aside from her fellow founders, Shirley enjoyed the relationships she had with other women who were a part of the early LPGA days. Not only were they accomplished golfers, many excelled in other sports such as baseball and tennis. Though it was the Tour that initially brought them together, it was their love of the game that sealed lifelong friendships. Sharing their knowledge of golf with the masses became a passion that would keep their lives intertwined for years and years to come.

Shirley Englehorn

Shirley Englehorn lived on a little 9-hole golf course in Caldwell, Idaho. As a teenager, she won several amateur tournaments in Idaho and Washington.

Shirley joined Betsy Rawls who was giving an exhibition in Boise, Idaho. They charged an appearance fee and people in the community gave Shirley's portion to her father to preserve her amateur status. It provided her some money to travel and be able to compete.

Shirley played in the 1959 Spokane Open. In most "Opens"

both pros and amateurs competed. Beverly Hanson won it, playing as a pro, and Shirley finished as low amateur. The tournament was held at the newly-opened Esmeralda Golf Course. It was another one of the courses that the LPGA Tour helped put on the map.

Shirley was 18 years old and had just graduated from high school. I was teaching at Tamarisk Country Club, and the Athletic Round Table wanted my opinion on whether or not they should sponsor her for the next three years. I thought Shirley had a lot of potential. She ended up turning pro and signed a contract with the Athletic Round Table. That same group had sponsored the first U.S. Women's Open in 1946 using profits from slot machines which they operated in a major hotel in Spokane. They had a long history with women's golf. The Athletic Round Table used their money and influence to bring professional sports to Spokane and gave money to deserving athletes.

"Little" Shirley, as she came to be known, arrived in Los Angeles on a Greyhound bus with her suitcase and her clubs. Her golf bag had a horse on it which was the logo of the Esmeralda Golf Course. My good friend, Jane Woolley, picked her up at the bus station and drove her to Palm Desert.

Little Shirley stayed with me all winter. I took her to Tamarisk with me every day. While I taught, she hit balls and then more balls. She played round after round with the members and then after playing, she'd return to the driving range and hit more balls. Then it was off to the putting green to hit putt after putt.

1959. "Little Shirley" Englehorn and "Big Shirley" Spork.

When January came, she was off to the East Coast to start her career on the LPGA Tour. The fifth tournament that season was the Titleholders Championship at Augusta Country Club. Augusta Country Club is an errant golf shot away from Augusta National where the Master's Tournament is held. By 1960, the Titleholders was a tournament for professionals only – it was no longer open for amateurs. It was the second week of March, and I wasn't there since I was busy teaching.

There was a freak snowstorm on Friday, so they canceled the second round. Several players were invited to a club member's ranch in a small town in South Carolina, which was just over the state line from Augusta, Georgia.

Little Shirley decided to ride a horse, that unbeknownst to her, hadn't been ridden all winter. She got on, and the horse bolted. It ran under a tree, and a large branch hit Shirley in the head. She fell back, and the horse fell on top of her. She suffered a concussion and broke her back in several places!

As you might guess, Little Shirley ended up in the hospital. She was placed in a semi-cast and in a bed that rotated 360 degrees every 24 hours. The doctor told her not only would she never play golf again, there was a good chance that she'd taken her last steps.

One day a nurse called me and said, "This child needs an adult here!" The nurse said they had called Shirley's parents and they couldn't come. "You are next on her list."

This was in March which was my busiest time of the year. I called my dear friend, Jane, and said, "Little Shirley needs me. I need to take a Red Eye flight from Los Angeles. I'll stay a day or two and then fly back. Can you go with me?"

Jane was able to get away and traveled with me. We visited Little Shirley for the weekend and stayed with the family who had been housing her for the tournament. The man was a member of Augusta National Golf Club. His name was C.C. Johnson, and he looked like Colonel Sanders. He owned the Cadillac dealership and the post office building. C.C. was very involved in golf and loved the game. He had been instrumental in securing Cadillac as a national sponsor for the Professional Golf Association (PGA). Because of that, PGA Tour and Club professionals could purchase a Cadillac at a huge discount. This later rolled over to LPGA Tour players.

A month later, C.C. called and said, "Somebody has to come down here and get this girl." Jane tried to explain to him that we weren't related, just friends, but that didn't seem to matter.

Back then, to get a person released from the hospital, you had to pay their bill, so I took up a collection from the members at Tamarisk for Little Shirley.

Jane and I again took the Red Eye out of Los Angeles. We went to the airport to catch our flight at 11:00 p.m. There were all kinds of problems with the plane, but we finally headed out. As we were taxiing toward the runway, I looked out the window. There was a telephone hanging down off the wing! I told the flight attendant. "Oh there is," she said as she looked out my window. Mechanics had been working on something, and they had left it plugged into the wing. We had to taxi back to the gate to disconnect the telephone which was yet another delay!

We finally taxied to the runway again and were beginning our ascent when the woman sitting in front of me gets up and says she thinks her sister is having a heart attack! The flight attendant told her to sit down — "Lady we're taking off." Once we were airborne, the flight attendant got on the intercom and asked if there was a doctor on the plane. Thankfully, there was, and he was able to take care of the situation.

On the aisle and a few seats up was a man who was blind. He buzzed the flight attendant and said he was diabetic and needed an insulin shot. The attendant led him back to the restroom and gave him the shot. This was all during one flight, just to get there! We finally arrived in Atlanta, and C.C. Johnson met us with his private plane. He was a pilot and flew us from Atlanta to Augusta.

PGA Tour player, Lloyd Mangrum, was on Golfcraft's staff and had heard about Shirley's accident through Jane. Jane's father owned Golfcraft, and Jane managed the pros who endorsed Golf-craft equipment. Lloyd visited Little Shirley while she was in the hospital and also convinced Ben Hogan to stop in and see her. Years before, Ben had been in a horrible car accident. He, too, was told that he'd never play golf again but worked his way back out on the PGA Tour the following year. I think Ben's visit was the shot in the arm that Little Shirley needed. He gave her hope.

When Jane and I arrived, we went to the hospital and paid Little Shirley's bill. She was in a brace from her neck to her knees but, with some assistance, was able to walk out of that hospital with us. We all headed back to the Johnson's home. Jane and I had to lay Little Shirley on a bed to get the brace on and off. Lifting her up took both of us! There was no way she could have done any of that by herself.

Before all this happened, Jane and I didn't even know C.C., his wife Laura, and the rest of the family. They treated us as if we'd been friends for years. I was only there a few days before heading home and back to work. Jane stayed with them and took care of Little Shirley. She became good friends with the Johnson family.

C.C. was quite a golfer, so Jane had her father make him a custom golf bag as a small gesture of thanks for all they had done for Little Shirley. That bag traveled all over with C.C., including several trips to the Bing Crosby Golf Tournament here in California.

When Little Shirley was well enough to travel, C.C. flew her and Jane in his plane to Atlanta so they could catch a direct flight to Los Angeles. I still can't believe all that the Johnson family, especially C.C., did to help us out during this difficult time.

Once they arrived back in Los Angeles, Little Shirley stayed at Jane's apartment, and Jane took care of her. Finally, Jane needed to get back to work. She went down to a store to use a pay phone, so Little Shirley couldn't hear her and talked to Shirley's father. This was way before the days of cell phones. Jane convinced him to come and take Little Shirley home so she could be around family while she recovered. That call convinced Little Shirley's father to pick her up and drive her back home to Idaho.

Little Shirley was not able to play golf again for some time but worked hard on conditioning and regaining her strength. When she was strong enough, she came back to the desert, and we worked on getting her ready for competition. A little over two years after the accident, she won her first tournament as a pro — the Lady Carling Eastern Open in Massachusetts in July of 1962. That September she also won the Eugene Open up in Oregon. Her determination and youth were instrumental in helping her bounce back — a miracle for sure!

She had won four tournaments before her second accident. At that time, the LPGA gave each of the top 10 money winners use of an Oldsmobile Starfire for a year. It had the LPGA emblem and the player's name on the door. Little Shirley was in the top 10 on the money list, so she had use of an LPGA-sponsored car for a year. She was on her way to the first tournament of the 1965 season in St. Petersburg, Florida. Sandra Palmer was riding with Shirley. They were between Phoenix and Tucson when the car's tie rod broke. Shirley couldn't steer it, and the car veered into the middle of the road. It kept hitting divider posts and driving the engine back toward her left foot. It broke several bones in her foot, shattered her ankle, and injured her hip. Miraculously, Sandra wasn't hurt.

Little Shirley had just been elected as president of the Tour for the 1965 season. She told them that as soon as she got out of the hospital in Tucson, she'd be at the events even though she couldn't play. The LPGA decided that wouldn't work and voted her out which I thought was rather a slap in the face.

Little Shirley always had that "I'll show you" attitude. When

I was teaching her, I would say, "You can't hit that shot!"

"I'll show you how I can hit that shot," she'd answer. Then she'd do it because that's just who she was. Little Shirley was always determined, competitive, and a great talent.

Again, Little Shirley worked her way back onto the Tour. Her first win, this second time around, was the 1966 Babe Zaharias Open in May. It was a 54-hole tournament and the second round was rained out. They played 36 holes on the final day and Little Shirley, bad ankle and all, beat Kathy Whitworth for the win by two strokes.

Little Shirley went on to win six more tournaments in the next four years including the LPGA Championship in 1970. At the end of every round, she had to ice her foot and her hip.

I once said that she could have been the next Babe Zaharias. She had every shot there was, and if it hadn't been for her accidents, Little Shirley would have probably been one of the Tour's top three golfers in the 1960s.

Little Shirley's competitive career was cut short because of the terrible accidents. After she retired from the Tour, I gave her the list of students who I had taught during the summer at the Westwood Diving Range in Los Angeles. Later, she taught at Rancho Park Golf Course which is also in L.A. Little Shirley lived with Jane while teaching at Westwood and Rancho Park. Then she moved to the Palm Springs area and taught at Desert Island Golf and Country Club. She later became the head pro and was there for years.

Gil Mombach had a sister who was a member of Desert Island. Gil talked to Little Shirley about starting a golf school for women only. She agreed to host and be the director of the new school. They held several sessions the next couple of years. Gil later approached me and asked if I would take over the school. I told him I would have to talk with Little Shirley. I needed her permission since I wouldn't step over her. Little Shirley was so busy, and I believe she was relieved to have one less responsibility. I got her blessing, and that's how I became the director of The School of Golf for Women Only for the next 20-plus years.

Presently, Little Shirley teaches at Kissing Camels at Garden of the Gods Club and Resort in Colorado. She taught the daughter of Donald Trump's lawyer when he and his family visited Colorado Springs. I believe her name was Kimberly. Kimberly was young and didn't really know what she wanted to do. In the winter they would fly Little Shirley to Florida and give her a place to live. All she had to do was work with Kimberly. Kimberly liked golf for about two years. Then she didn't like it anymore, so that was the end of Little Shirley being at Trump International and playing golf with "The Donald" in her leisure time.

Little Shirley was LPGA National Teacher of the Year in 1978 and was inducted into the LPGA Teaching Hall of Fame in 2014. We go back a lot of years, and it was my honor to be her presenter at the ceremony.

She still has the grit, determination, and compassion for golf

. . . a game which we all love and cherish.

Jackie Pung

Jackie Pung's father was Hawaiian, and her mother was French, German, and Irish. She grew up in Hawaii and worked at Sears and Roebuck. Jackie later married Barney, who was a fireman on a Standard Oil Company tanker, and they had two daughters – Barnette and Leilani.

Jackie became interested in golf at a young age and became serious when she was a high school sophomore. She won the Hawaiian Women's Amateur Championship four times. Her first crown was in 1938, and her last was in 1947.

Jackie met Babe Zaharias and Babe's husband, George, in 1938. They had stopped over in Hawaii on their way to Australia. Babe was going to play some exhibitions in Australia. After seeing Jackie's golf swing, Babe invited her to tag along, but Jackie's parents said, "No!"

In 1952, Jackie traveled to the mainland and played in the U.S. Women's Amateur at Waverley Country Club in Portland, Oregon. She won the tournament and afterwards performed a hula dance on the 18th green. This was her way of thanking and honoring the United States Golf Association (USGA) and the staff at Waverley Country Club. Officials from the USGA scolded her for this because they didn't understand her Hawaiian culture. There was an immediate outcry from the public and the press. They all defended her and

Jackie was allowed to perform her hula from then on.

A few months later, Jackie turned pro and signed a contract with MacGregor Golf Company. They sent her to take lessons from Tommy Armour in Boca Raton, Florida. He called her the "Date Nut Palm," because she was square like a box — five foot two or three and over 200 pounds. I don't know why, but Tommy didn't like working with Jackie. He turned her over to his assistant who helped her with her game and taught her how to give clinics for MacGregor.

Jackie traveled on the LPGA Tour with her two teenage daughters in the mid-1950s. She played in the 1957 U.S. Women's Open at Winged Foot Country Club in New York and won the tournament. On the final day, Jackie was teamed with Betty Jameson. Back then, your playing partner kept your scorecard. Jackie shot a 72 in the final round, but Betty wrote the wrong score on the fourth hole. She had written down a "5" when Jackie had actually taken a "6." Even with her "6," she still would have won.

The press was all over Jackie because they knew she had won. She signed the card without checking it. Jackie had simply written over the top of the scores Betty had recorded. The total was correct, but because the score on that one hole was wrong, she was disqualified. This gave Betsy Rawls the title and $1,800 in first-place prize money. The country club members at Winged Foot were very upset! They took up a collection because they didn't think it was fair. Jackie ended up with over $3,000, which was more than she would have received if she had won, but she still lost the title of U.S. Women's

Open Champion.

Because of this, the USGA changed the score cards. They added a tear off along the bottom of the card so players could record their score hole by hole. It's still used today on the Tours.

Personally, I don't think you should have to keep your own score in a professional tournament. I think it should be done by an official scorekeeper. It's too much when you have the press and gallery all over you as you walk off the 18th green. If you notice in today's tournaments, the winner is escorted to the scoring tent first. The press has to wait until the card is signed and submitted. Much of this is a direct result of Jackie's disaster at the 1957 U.S. Women's Open.

Jackie and I had traveled together one summer in the early 1960s. She loved jelly-filled doughnuts and ice cream. When we'd see a doughnut or ice cream shop, she'd have me stop. While I was driving, she was eating.

In the early years of the Tour, there were no golf clothes. No skirts with pockets. The Simplicity Company had a pattern for culottes that had pockets and one for a gaucho-type skirt. In the '50s, it was a new thing to have a shirt or blouse that had buttons. Most of the time we wore a print top and a plain bottom. We bought material and took it to a seamstress to have our clothes made. Jackie, however, could sew and made her own clothes. There was so much more variety of printed fabrics on the mainland than in Hawaii, so at every tournament stop, we would make a special trip to the local fabric store. As we headed down the road, we were filling the car with more and more bolts of patterned fabric that Jackie bought.

Our Tour stops were taking us from the Midwest towards California. Everywhere we went, Jackie seemed to find something she loved and couldn't live without. We stopped somewhere in New Mexico and had enchiladas. Jackie loved them, so she bought a case of enchilada sauce to send home.

Finally, when we left New Mexico, we had to rent a U-Haul for all of Jackie's "treasures" since we had run out of room in the car. We still had two more tournaments before we arrived in California, and there we were pulling a U-Haul merrily down the road.

During our stop in Phoenix, we were staying at the home of a woman doctor. We had to back the U-Haul into her driveway. We ended up unhooking the trailer and pushing it into the driveway, because I couldn't back it in. I am the worst backer-upper!

When we finally arrived in Palm Desert, one of Jackie's daughters, who was working for a rental car company in San Francisco, met us. She helped us transfer all of Jackie's purchases into the rental car, and off they went. They drove back to the Bay Area where all of Jackie's possessions were loaded onto the tanker which her husband Barney worked on. Then Barney, and all of Jackie's "treasures," sailed back to Hawaii.

Jackie retired from the LPGA Tour in 1964 after 11 years. She headed back to Hawaii where she taught for years. In 1967, three years after she returned to the Island, Jackie was voted LPGA

Teacher of the Year.

Althea Gibson

Althea Gibson was the first African-American woman on the
LPGA Tour, playing from 1964 to 1978. When we played the U.S.
Women's Open in Oklahoma, the tournament site had a "White
Only" policy in their clubhouse. If Althea couldn't go in, the rest of
us wouldn't either. We all changed our shoes in the car. We were a
small group, but we were a family, and we stuck together.

Being Hawaiian, Jackie Pung also had dark skin, and many of
the places where we stopped thought she was black. We were turned
away from several motels and diners. When that happened, we just
got back in our cars and headed on down the road. We encountered
a lot of prejudice in the early days of the Tour. Some of the discrimination was race-based, while other was just because we were women.
However, unlike the men's PGA Tour, our Tour never had a "Cauca-
sian-Only Clause." The LPGA never excluded **any** woman from the
day it was formed!

Althea picked up golf late in life after a tremendously successful tennis career. While we were starting the LPGA Tour in the 1950s,
she was breaking down racial barriers in the tennis world. Althea was
the first African American to play at Wimbledon in 1951 and to win
the French Open in 1956. She went on to win both the women's
singles and doubles titles at Wimbledon, as well as the Women's U.S.
National Championship (now known as the U.S. Open) in 1957

and 1958. Both years she was the number-one ranked women's tennis player in both the United States and the World.

The Associated Press named Althea Female Athlete of the Year in both 1957 and 1958, and she was also the first African-American woman to appear on the cover of both *Sports Illustrated* and *Time* magazines.

In golfing circles, Virginia Van Wie was the first woman to be named Athlete of the Year by the Associated Press back in 1934. Women's golf first found its way onto the cover of *Time* in 1924 thanks to the great amateur Edith Cummings, while Barbara Romack was the first to appear on *Sports Illustrated* in 1956. Barbara had a great amateur career and had not planned on turning pro, but in 1958 Fred Corcoran convinced her to join our Tour. Women's golf is second only to women's tennis for producing the most Associated Press Female Athletes of the Year.

Alice Marble, who won 12 U.S. Opens and five Wimbledon titles, was instrumental in opening up the tennis world for Althea. Alice reprimanded her sport for not including **all** great players. Speaking of Alice, later in life she moved to the Palm Springs area, and we became friends. Not only was she a great athlete who dominated her sport, but she was a very interesting person. Alice had a photographic memory and was recruited by our government to be a spy during World War II. She got shot in the back while on a mission in Switzerland.

Actress, Carole Lombard, was one of her good friends. Alice

gave lessons to many of the rich and famous including William du Pont, Jr., who was an avid tennis player. He and his wife divorced in 1941, and six years later William married the famous tennis champion, Margaret Osborne, who was one of Alice's successors. Alice's biography, *Courting Danger,* is very good if you like biographies.

Although Althea dominated tennis in the 1950s, she couldn't make a living at it. She didn't turn pro until 1959 when she was already 37 years old. Althea left the tennis world shortly afterward. She took up golf seriously and joined the LPGA Tour in 1964 which just goes to show what an incredible athlete she was.

After dominating her sport, Althea found it difficult to compete against women who had played golf for years. Althea was up against Marilynn Smith, Betsy Rawls, Marlene Hagge, Mary Lena Faulk, Clifford Ann Creed, Mary Mills, Ruth Jessen, Sandra Haynie, Carol Mann, Shirley Englehorn, Kathy Whitworth, and Mickey Wright. With a strong field like that, it's not surprising that she never won on the LPGA Tour, but she did finish tied for second at the 1970 Len Immke Buick Open in Columbus, Ohio. She was in a three-way playoff with Mary Mills and Sandra Haynie. Sandra was eliminated on the first playoff hole, and Mary beat Althea on the following hole.

Althea was a talented vocalist and saxophonist and, like Babe Zaharias, appeared on the *Ed Sullivan Show.* She was also a regular on the popular television show *What's My Line.* In her final years, she struggled with her health. Althea also had financial issues which was sadly a reflection of the prejudice of the times.

Renee Powell

Althea was followed by Renee Powell who joined the LPGA Tour three years later in 1967. Renee was born and raised in East Canton, Ohio; and like Althea, is African American.

Renee's father, William (Bill), was a golfer. He went to Wilberforce University and played on the golf team. Later, he served in Europe during World War II and was stationed in Scotland and England. On his days off, Bill often played golf. He walked the legendary holes of some very famous golf courses . . . courses that were more concerned about your golf score than the color of your skin.

When Bill came back home, he was restricted since African Americans weren't allowed to play on many of the courses. Because of that, he decided to build his own golf course on an old dairy farm, modeling the holes after ones he remembered playing in Scotland and England. The first nine holes were opened in 1948, and 30 years later, a second nine was added. Bill was the first African American to build, own, and operate a golf course. That course, Clearview Golf Club, in East Canton, is now listed on the National Registry of Historic Places. Every year Renee and her brother, Larry, host a pro-am at their family's course. I've been blessed to attend this event the past several years.

Renee traveled with Sandra Post on the Tour. They had met at the 1962 U.S. Girls' Junior Championship. Sandra was only 14 years old and the only Canadian who competed in the championship. She and Renee have been friends ever since. Tour life was tough, and Renee faced a lot of discrimination from golf courses, restaurants, and motels. Sandra ran interference for Renee, checking them into their motel rooms, but she couldn't shield her from all of it. When they would be turned away, Sandra would joke that it was because she was Canadian.

In 1979, Renee became the first woman head golf professional in England. It was at Silvermere Golf Course near London. About a year later, she returned home and began developing an inner-city youth golf program in Cleveland. She helped establish The First Tee, a program designed to introduce the game of golf to junior girls. For years, Renee was the development/programming consultant at The First Tee headquarters in St. Augustine, Florida. To this day, she is still active, focusing on introducing the game to disadvantaged girls.

Renee is one of only a few women on the Pro Football Hall of Fame Board of Trustees. The Museum (in Canton, Ohio) is close to her golf course.

Renee received an Honorary Doctorate of Laws degree from the University of St Andrews, Scotland in 2008. Her father was still alive and got to go with her.

In February of 2015, after 260 years in existence, the Royal and Ancient Golf Club opened its membership to women. Louise Suggs, Annika Sorenstam, Laura Davies, Lally Segard, Belle Robertson, Princess Anne, and Renee Powell were the first women invited to join this prestigious club as honorary members. Renee has seen quite a change in her life — from being denied access to some courses, to being one of the first seven women members at the course where the game of golf started.

It's been said that history repeats itself. In 1951, I was given a tour through the Royal and Ancient Clubhouse — including the men's locker room. Some 64 years later, Renee found herself in that same room. While she was standing there, she noticed the name Powell on one of the locker plates and said, "I wonder if that person is related to me."

The attendant answered, "No ma'am, that's your locker!"

Renee is the most gentle, accepting, non-judgmental, forgiving person I've ever known and is much deserving of all the recognition she's received. I'm proud to be included in her circle of friends.

Joanne Winter

Joanne was born in Chicago. Her mother died when she was very young, and her father trained boxers – not the dogs, the fighters. Joanne and her brother grew up in the city park system. At the end of the school day, she went to the park and played marbles, horseshoes, and baseball. She also spent time at the gym where her father worked. Because of her upbringing, she was an accomplished athlete in several sports.

Joanne dropped out of high school to play semi-pro softball. She was a pitcher. Women's softball was big in the 1940s and drew good-sized crowds.

Joanne, her brother, and her father moved to Phoenix because her father's health was bad. He needed to get out of the Chicago winters. When Joanne heard about the formation of the All-American Girls Professional Baseball League (AAGPBL) in 1943, she returned to Chicago to try out.

The AAGPBL was the brainstorm of Phillip K. Wrigley who inherited the chewing gum empire and the Chicago Cubs baseball team from his father. It was exciting to see the Cubs break the 108-year "curse" and win the 2016 World Series. Joanne would have loved that. Wrigley started the girls league because the men were fighting in the war. The tryouts were held at Wrigley Field. Over 500 girls showed up, and Joanne was one of the 60 girls chosen to play. There were four teams. Joanne was assigned to the Racine Belles. She played eight seasons for the Belles up in Racine, Wisconsin.

1946 was Joanne's best year. The size of the ball they played with was larger than a baseball and smaller than a softball, but she still threw 17 shutouts, six in a row, that season. The Racine Belles beat the Rockford Peaches for the league crown. Joanne pitched a shutout in the final game, and the Belles won 1-0 in 14 innings!

Penny Marshall's movie, *A League of Their Own*, had the Peaches beating the Belles for the championship, but that wasn't what happened. While filming the movie, Penny had invited several of the surviving players (which included Joanne) to be on set as advisors. Joanne wasn't at all happy when the movie had her team losing the championship game to their arch rival.

During the time she was playing ball, Joanne started a candy company called Joanne Winter Chocolates. She hired a lady to teach her how to dip chocolates which have to be turned and twisted a certain way. Joanne sold the candy at local gift shops wrapped in Christmas paper. She would pick up what didn't sell during the holiday season and rewrap it with Valentine's Day paper, and then Easter paper. It was her sideline business and helped her make ends meet.

After her baseball career was over, Joanne moved back to Phoenix and went to work for Motorola. Later, she got a job teaching tennis at the Biltmore Hotel. The Wrigley's owned the Biltmore. Phillip Wrigley, who had started the women's baseball league, helped Joanne get the job. She taught tennis to all the movie stars who vacationed there.

During this time, Joanne took up golf and later taught both tennis and golf. She won the Arizona State Women's Amateur Golf Championship and then joined the LPGA Tour in 1962. She only played a few years until 1965. Joanne retired due to flare-ups from a previous back injury she had suffered in a car accident.

Joanne settled in Scottsdale and taught at a practice range and 9-hole course. She coached at the community college and later at Arizona State University (ASU). Joanne worked with several future LPGA Tour players: Danielle Ammaccapane, Jerilyn Britz, Julie Stanger Pyne, Heather Farr, and Alice Miller, just to name a few.

I met Joanne in Kalamazoo, Michigan and later got to know

her when I started the LPGA teaching section in the western states. She had a cabin in the Payson area which is above Scottsdale. During the weekends in the summer, she would go there to cool off. She suggested that I come over, bring some students, and we'd start a golf school. There are a lot of crystals in the area that look like diamonds, so we named our school "Diamonds in the Rough." Some of Joanne's friends who lived nearby made plaques with crystals on them so our students would have a memento of their trip to Payson.

Our schools were fun. People wanted to come out and enjoy themselves, as well as learn. During the day we taught, and at night we took our students to the bars, line danced, and all sorts of stuff.

We held our schools in August when it's hot in the desert. Payson is about 90 miles northeast of Phoenix and much cooler since the elevation is almost 5,000 feet. At that time, Payson only had one golf course, and it was nine holes.

Our school grew, so we added Judy Whitehouse to our teaching staff. She was a good golfer and a past Arizona Women's Amateur Golf Champion. Judy lived in Phoenix, and like Joanne and me, needed somewhere to go to get out of the heat in the summer.

Joanne had coached the Arizona State University (ASU) team for one season, but it was too much for her with everything else she was doing, so she resigned. Judy coached the ASU team from 1975 to 1978.

Joanne was a great teacher and taught for over 30 years. She would say that the golf swing was two turns and two steps, "You turn and step on your back foot. Then you turn and step on your front foot." She also said that the tempo of a golf swing was like, "A penguin walking down a railroad track swinging a watermelon."

I ran The School of Golf for Women Only at Singing Hills Golf Course in El Cajon, California. The owner of the school, Gil Mombach, roasted me on my 65th birthday. It was a takeoff of the old television show; *This is Your Life*. Gil surprised me by bringing in several of my long-time friends. Wouldn't you know, Joanne came through the door swinging her watermelon.

In 1971, Joanne started the Arizona Silver Belle Golf Championship for girls from the ages of 13 to 23. The tournament is still going strong and is a nice legacy Joanne left behind.

When the LPGA Teaching Division introduced the title of master professional, Joanne was one of the 14 in the inaugural class. She was named Teacher of the Year in 1969 and received the LPGA Ellen Griffin Rolex Award in 1995, the year before she died.

I knew Joanne for a lot of years. She was a cherished colleague and a dear, dear friend.

I remember when I met you at Esmeralda Golf Course in Spokane, Washington. You asked me to come to California and work on my golf game. I met Jane Woolley and my professional career began. You spent countless hours teaching me how to improve my golf game as well as how to teach sound basics: grip, setup, backswing, and follow through to a balanced position at the finish. I will never forget that knowledge and have used it throughout my teaching career.

The best shot making — hitting the golf ball with spin — I've ever seen was at Macktown Golf Course in Rockton, Illinois. I was playing with you, and the spin you put on the ball was awesome. You hit the ball so pure — it looked like it was climbing up each step of a ladder in slow motion. The ball floated through the air and dropped to the ground like a feather; ever so lightly. I had never seen that before and never will again.

All of your students are proud of you, especially me. Your dedication to the game has inspired golfers and made them better people no matter what they choose to do in life.

Thank you Pro, for all those long hours and wonderful memories. I will love you forever!

Shirley Englehorn a.k.a. "Little Shirley"
LPGA Tour - Life Member
LPGA Teaching & Club Professional - Master Life Member
LPGA Teaching & Club Professional - Hall of Fame

As a young 21-year-old Montana girl who had recently arrived in San Diego, California, I was encouraged by a co-worker to attend an LPGA Teaching Seminar. In my wildest dreams, I could not have envisioned sitting in a room full of women with such great teaching and golfing accomplishments. The obvious glue to all of these independent women was sitting in the center, Shirley Spork. She approached me, and I was mortified of what stupid utterance I might blurt out to a "legend." Thirty-eight years later, she is my mentor, my friend, and my most cherished teacher of golf and life.

Shirley's interest in learning has never waned; whether it is a new swing theory, a method of teaching or just plain "life stuff." I'll never forget Shirley's most recent visit to Montana. We had special back-stage access to the state rodeo. Shirley had both hands glued to the tall corral fence with her nose sticking through like a ten-year-old kid. A big ol' bull broke out of the gate, not five yards from where she was standing. He thrashed and bucked right in front of her, pelting her with chunks of mud. Anyone else would have backed away from that fence out of mortal fear of the snorting, drooling, very angry bull, but not Shirley. She was soaking it all in. Fearless. Excited. She was learning.

Connie Cramer Caouette
LPGA Teaching & Club Professional - Class "A" Life Member
Head Golf Professional - Eagle Falls & Anaconda Hills Golf Courses,
Great Falls, Montana

HOLE # 9

Fishing Stories

It's funny. When you ask people what their favorite pastime is, many will say golf. When you ask a golf pro what their favorite recreation activity is, many will say fishing. Nowhere is this truer than in Shirley's life. Fishing was a passion. She fished anywhere and anytime her scheduled allowed.

I have always loved to fish from as far back as I can remember. Didn't matter what kind: ocean, lake, or river. I just loved holding a fishing pole, waiting for that big strike. I bought my first fishing rod when I was 10 years old. The company that made Popsicles had a promotion — send in five Popsicle sticks and 25 cents and they'd send you a fishing rod. So as soon as I'd eaten my five Popsicles, that's what I did.

Some of my favorite fishing memories are from when I was the head pro at a golf course in Ukiah, California. Occasionally I took a day off and drove to The Narrows; which is part of Clear Lake. I would take my lunch, rent a rowboat, and spend my day fishing. I enjoy lake fishing. It's very relaxing — sitting in a boat and dangling a line in the water. Thinking about the fish . . . how big it is, where it is, and is it going to take your bait?

The scenery was beautiful with the mountains seeming to touch the water's edge. Whether or not I caught any fish, I considered myself very fortunate to be able to enjoy such a peaceful, relaxing day.

Shirley Englehorn, whom we had nicknamed "Little Shirley" when she first came to Palm Desert, to work on her golf game with me, is from Idaho. After about a year, she said, "You've got to come to Idaho so we can go fishing. I want to take you fishing!" I even had a very famous J.C. Higgins, Shirley Englehorn-endorsed, powder-blue rod/reel and fishing tackle box from Sears & Roebuck. It had a mirror on the inside of the lid. Very fancy for sure!

My housemate, Jane Woolley, and I drove to Idaho. Once we arrived at Little Shirley's, she couldn't wait to take us to one of her favorite streams. As we walked to the car, Little Shirley told us she had brought her gun. I asked, "Why do we need a gun?"

"Well," she said, "in case we see a rattlesnake or something."

We drove to hell-and-gone on this gravel road to reach the stream. It was the time of year when rattlesnakes shed their skins. As we drove down the road, we saw all these snake skins hanging on farm fences. We dropped Jane off down by a bridge where she'd be safe. We drove a little farther, parked the car, grabbed our fishing gear, and then walked through this field. As we headed to the river bank, my eyes were racing back and forth looking for rattlesnakes, but not Little Shirley. She was just walking along like she didn't have a care in the world.

Once we got to the stream, it didn't take long for Little Shirley to land her limit of rainbow trout. That girl can catch fish anywhere! I was too nervous, so I really wasn't enjoying our outing. Once we finished fishing, we headed back through the field. As we got near the car, I heard this hissing sound and thought, "Oh, my God, it's a rattlesnake! I hope she can shoot it!"

It wasn't a snake; it was one of my car tires going flat. Thank God I had a spare. The two of us changed that tire in record speed and got the heck out of there. We picked up Jane from the bridge and headed back to Little Shirley's where her mother cooked us a delicious fish dinner.

Another time, Little Shirley and I had just finished playing a pro-am in Oklahoma. Two of the pro-am players came up and asked us if we would like to go fishing.

"Oh yeah, we love to fish," we answered.

The next night they picked us up at our motel and drove us to a lake a few miles away. We walked down to the boat, and one of the guys is carrying a battery.

I asked, "What do you need an extra battery for?"

He said, "Sometimes we have trouble with the one in the boat, and we want to be safe out there."

"Well okay," we thought, "safety is important."

They set the battery on the floor of the boat. There was a great big net with a long wooden handle and a half of a baseball bat sitting in the boat . . . but **no** fishing poles.

After we pushed away from shore, they asked, "How big of a fish do you want? Twenty pounds, 30 pounds — how big?"

"Big!" we answered.

So off we went, Little Shirley and me in the front of the boat and these two guys in the back. We get toward the middle of the lake and one guy says, "Are you all set?"

And I say, "Yeah, sure."

So he tells us to get the net ready. He said, "Now count to 15. When you see the fish, one of you girls scoop it out of the water with the net and dump it in the boat. The other one take the bat and whack it in the head."

We thought this was crazy, but we started counting — a thousand one, a thousand two, and so on until a thousand 15. Sure enough here comes this huge fish! We netted it and got it into the boat. Little Shirley and I took turns swinging at this thing trying to kill it. Catfish are ugly with their whiskers, but we were so excited about the size of this fish — a 35-pound catfish!

What they had done was taken the extra battery and thrown the negative and positive ends into the water. It stuns the fish and brings them to the surface, but the fish recover quickly, so you have to be fast with the net.

We went back to shore and got out of the boat. They took

that fish and nailed it to the side of the cabin garage. Then took a pair of pliers and skinned it. They gave it to us, and we took it back to the motel where we were staying. Lucky for us, there was a coffee shop connected to our motel. The kitchen prepared it and served it all week. Any of our fellow golfers who wanted catfish could have it for lunch and dinner. It was delicious — this beautiful white fish.

Little Shirley and I were telling one of the locals about our adventure, and they asked who had taken us fishing. We told them who it was, and it turns out that one of them was the game warden! It was the most illegal thing you can do — throw a battery charge in the water to make the fish come up. But we did. Naive, young ladies!

There was a time that Jane and I were camping in our RV near a stream in Sun Valley, Idaho, when a hatchery truck came and dumped a full load of trout. We caught enough to eat for breakfast, lunch, and dinner for four days, and we could even share with our fellow campers. Lucky us!

Many of the golfers on both the LPGA and the PGA Tour used to carry fishing gear in a case in their golf bag. They had a collapsible rod and a few lures. Some courses we played had a lake where we could go out and fish. That's what Johnny Miller and several other pros used to do when they played the Tour. They would go out with their kids, catch-and-release; or if it was allowed, keep the fish and take it to the hotel chef for him to cook for their dinner. It was a relaxing hobby.

In October 1952, I received a sponsor invitation to play in

September, 1966. Joan Wulff giving Shirley a fly fishing lesson
at The Lodge at Jackson Hole, Wyoming.

the Northern California-Reno Open which was a PGA tournament. I was the only woman to play with the men pros. The course played long for me since I played from men's tees, but I still shot a 77 in the opening round. Once the round was over, a few of us headed to the Truckee River to fish. We waded out into the icy water and caught some beautiful rainbow trout. We took our catch to a local restaurant, and the chef cooked it. It was delicious! What a wonderful way to celebrate getting to play in a PGA event.

1970s. Shirley and a BIG rainbow trout that took patience to land during a rainstorm in West Yellowstone, Montana.

I caught my first Dolly Varden trout, also known as a bull trout, with my new fly rod in a narrow stream in the middle of a meadow in Sargents, Colorado. Jane and Little Shirley were there with me fishing. That was very special.

Jane and I use to vacation in Victoria, British Columbia. We

211

would pack up our motorhome and head north for several weeks in the summer to escape the desert heat.

For several years I was the director of a golf school in Rancho Santa Fe, California. If there was a school while we were on vacation, Jane would stay with the motorhome and our dogs, and I would fly to San Diego. Someone would pick me up at the airport; I would teach the school and then fly back to Victoria.

One year, I caught a beautiful big salmon. I called the chef who ran the restaurant at Whispering Palms Country Club where we held the school. He said, "Great, bring it down. I'd love to cook it." I packed it in dry ice and loaded it into my travel bag; along with my golf clubs. My salmon was the featured item on the menu for anyone attending the school. Travis was an amazing chef. He would come and take a bow after we had enjoyed feasting on his delicious dishes. That was probably some of the best salmon I've ever eaten, thanks to Travis.

Joan Wulff was one of my fishing mentors. She was born in 1926, a year before me, and is a legend in the fishing world! She competed against the men and was casting champion from 1943 to 1960.

Joan and her husband, Lee, started a fly fishing school in 1979 on the Beaverkill River in the Catskills in New York. Lee died in 1991. He was piloting a Piper Super Cub and crashed during a takeoff. The Wulff School of Fly Fishing is still running, but I'm not sure if Joan still teaches.

I met Joan in September of 1966 at The Lodge at Jackson Hole, Wyoming. The Lodge happened to be hosting the International Federation of Fly Fisher's Second Conclave. Joan was scheduled to give an exhibition, and I was there on a fishing vacation.

They had set up hula hoops — red, green, and yellow — in a trough of water about 100 feet long. Joan was going to be "presenting the fly" into each hoop.

My golf mentor and good friend, Joey Rey, was the golf pro at the Jackson Hole Golf Club. I had known Joey for a long time. Fifteen years earlier, he had invited me to teach with him at Pasatiempo Golf Club in Northern California and then helped me get my first head pro job in Ukiah. He came up with the bright idea that Joan and I should have a contest. I would pitch golf balls, and she would "present the fly," through the hoops. It was arranged for the end of the week. I paced off the distance to each hoop and then headed to the driving range. I had five days to practice.

Joan had been entertaining those attending the convention throughout the week. The day of the big contest arrived — golf versus fly fishing. Finally, it was time for our match, and I went first.

The center hoop was yellow. I said, "Yellow." My ball dropped right in the middle. Someone in the audience yelled, "Hit it again!" I was about to hit another shot to the yellow hoop when I heard this little voice, Babe's voice, in the back of my head saying, "Once you do it kid; don't do it again!" Instead of repeating that shot, I said, "Green," and that went right in. Then I called, "Red," the long one,

1970s. Marlin fishing in Cabo San Lucas, Mexico.

and it went in, too. I hit three perfect pitch shots.

It was a little breezy, and Joan had trouble hitting the hula hoops. There wasn't enough breeze to affect my golf ball, but there was just enough wind to blow her fly off course. I won, but only because it was too windy for Joan to present the fly. It helped that a golf ball is so much heavier than a fly.

After the contest, I stood on the grass and hit golf balls into the marshland where all the moose lived. There was a large audience. I talked about the sand wedge and showed them how to hit several shots. After the impromptu clinic, I gave Joan a lesson. She hit shots into the marsh, and then we headed to the swimming pool at the famous Jackson Hole Lodge. I stood on the diving board, and Joan gave me a fly casting lesson. It was a special time I'll never forget!

I went to Jackson Hole on several other memorable fly fishing trips. I can remember wading into the creek, falling down, taking off my wet clothes, and putting them on a bush to dry. I must admit though, I never really liked fly fishing. It's just too hard and very technical. You have to present the fly into a very, very small area where the fish are swimming. The hook has to be set just right, or the fish is gone. You have to use your whole shoulder when fly fishing. You've got to keep the line behind you and make sure it doesn't get snagged in a bush.

Jane and I used to practice at her condominium pool at Indian Wells Country Club. One time, a neighbor of Jane's saw us and said we were disrupting the pool!

I like spin casting the best. It's a lot easier because it can be flicked with the wrist and unlike fly fishing, doesn't take much practice.

I have done a little ocean fishing in Cabo San Lucas, Mexico. It was hard work landing the 135-pound marlin that I caught on 48-pound test line! The fish comes up, the line goes out, and then you reel some more. You have to have a great captain, because he has to chase the fish with the boat in reverse to keep slack in the line. It took me 50 minutes to land my fish, and my elbow hurt for a year which wasn't good for golf. That's a once in a lifetime event — I would never ever do it again.

I still enjoy fishing, but can't walk the streams or deep sea fish like I've done for so many years of my life. Golf was my life, but fishing was my favorite hobby.

Shirley catches her limit.

It's wonderful that Shirley Spork is writing about her life and experiences. She has a great story to tell and certainly a lot of history about the LPGA, which is so very important.

I joined the LPGA Tour in 1959 which as it turned out was the year Shirley, along with others, founded the LPGA Teaching Division.

I remember as I became a better player, being asked to participate in some of the golf schools being conducted by the teaching division. That's when I became more aware of Shirley and what they were trying to establish.

Just as Shirley helped the LPGA become a great Tour, she also helped make the LPGA Teaching & Club Professional Division (as it is known today) become one of most respected organizations in the golfing community.

It's been wonderful to see all the honors Shirley has received. They certainly are well-earned and deserved.

I'm quite sure anyone who reads this memoir will come away with a much better appreciation of who the founders were and what they accomplished.

Kathy Whitworth
LPGA Tour - Life Member
World Golf Hall of Fame

Shirley Spork has a wealth of knowledge of the game of golf and its history. She is an excellent communicator and shares her love of the game freely. She is an excellent raconteur and dinner party guest.

Three cheers for Shirley!

Amy Alcott
LPGA Tour - Life Member
LPGA Teaching & Club Professional - Honorary Member
World Golf Hall of Fame

HOLE # 10

The Ups and Downs
of Tour Life

In the 1960s and 1970s Shirley was managing golf courses and teaching, but still found time to play in several tournaments. Television was starting to make its mark on the Tour, and one of the most iconic LPGA tournaments was about to be born. New stars were emerging and traveling to wherever the tournament director could land a sponsor who was willing to host a tournament. Well after Y2K was a distant memory, many of the players had the opportunity to gather and reminisce about their time together on the Tour. Life doesn't get any better than when you can spend time with old friends.

There was a tournament where a bridge collapsed. It was in Mount Clemens, Michigan. We were playing the second round of the Women's Wolverine Open Golf Tournament at Hillcrest Country Club in July of 1963.

You had to hit your tee shot over the Clinton River on the 16th hole. Then you crossed a 200-foot long, pedestrian suspension bridge. It was about 18 feet above the river and had square chicken wire on both sides.

As I was walking to the 17th tee, I looked back down the 16th fairway. The group behind us had just teed off. There was a large crowd around the bridge. I bent over to tee up my ball, and when I stood back up all the people near the bridge were gone!

I turned around to my playing partners and said, "Where did everybody go?"

Then we heard somebody yell, "The bridge collapsed!"

A large gallery and an electric golf cart were on the bridge, and it was just too much weight. It twisted, creaked, and broke! The people on the bridge got tangled up in the chicken wire, and everything ended up in the river.

The water was only three to six feet deep, and everyone rushed into the river to pull people out. That's why they had all disappeared. My former boyfriend, Ben Lula, was the head pro at the course. Ben, who I had dated in high school, was right in the middle of the river helping people reach the shore.

Ruth Jessen was in the group behind us and was leading the tournament. She was playing with Marlene Bauer Hagge and Jo Ann Prentice. Ruth and Marlene had just gotten across, but Jo Ann was still on the bridge when it fell. Her caddy jumped in and pulled her to safety, but she was injured and taken away in an ambulance. I believe about 80 people fell into the river and around 50 were taken to various hospitals.

My group was in shock. We didn't know what to do. Should

we stop or keep playing? Lenny Wirtz, our tournament director, was there. He told us, "Just keep playing. Don't stop! You're going to be on TV!"

The state highway ran parallel to the 17th fairway. We had to walk off the course, through a ditch, and down the highway to get around the disaster. Ambulances were coming and going. This was in the early days of television for us, and the camera was on the 18th green, so we had to keep playing.

When we finally got to the 18th green, we didn't know if anyone was hurt. We were looking around, trying to figure out what was going on. All this while we were putting out. It was one great big mess!

When it was all over, they threw out everyone's second-round score. We replayed the second round the next day (Sunday), and the final round was held on Monday. Without the bridge, two of the holes were hard to reach, so we only played 16 holes the final two rounds. That was the only 50-hole tournament I ever remember playing, and Kathy Whitworth won it.

It was four months later, November 1963, when another, even greater, tragedy struck. President John F. Kennedy was assassinated.

Kathy Whitworth had grown up in the small town of Jal, New Mexico where her parents owned the local hardware store. Jal was a town of about 3,000 people, and Kathy had put them on the map. There was a huge billboard on the highway just outside of Jal that said, "Home of LPGA Professional, Kathy Whitworth." November 23 was to be "Kathy Whitworth Appreciation Day" along with a tournament.

Betty Hicks had flown her Beechcraft Bonanza to Palm Springs to pick up Shirley Englehorn and me. From there we flew to Phoenix to pick up Joanne Winter. We stayed the night in Phoenix and flew on to El Paso, Texas, the next day. There were four people, four sets of clubs, and four small suitcases; which was a real overload for that plane, but we arrived safely.

After landing, we took a cab to Juarez, Mexico, for lunch. We were also making a "rum run" to buy some liquor before flying on to Jal for Kathy's big day.

While we were having lunch in Juarez, all we heard on the radio was Kennedy this and Kennedy that. None of us spoke Spanish, so we didn't have a clue what they were talking about. We didn't know that President Kennedy had just been assassinated in Dallas.

Next thing we knew, the cab driver who had taken us to Juarez ran up to our table. He told us to stop eating, put some money on the table, and get in the cab! He had to get us back across the border before they closed it. And, sure enough, he was right. The border closed soon after our very perceptive cab driver got us back into the United States. I cannot imagine what would have happened, or how long we would have been stranded in Mexico.

We made it to Jal and played in the tournament, which Mickey Wright won. The Governor of New Mexico was supposed to be there but changed his plans after what had happened in Dallas. There's less than 400 miles between Jal and Dallas, so it was close to home. The Mayor of Jal ended up presenting Kathy with her award.

If you're over 53 years old, do you remember where you were when President Kennedy was shot? I was having lunch in Juarez, Mexico, with Joanne, Betty, and Little Shirley and we didn't get to make our liquor run. We were just in a hurry to get back across the border.

The first LPGA tournament held in Southern California was in 1953. It was called The Palm Springs Open and sponsored by one of the greatest supporters of the early Tour, Helen Lengfeld. It was played at Tamarisk Country Club, where I later taught, and Jackie Pung won it.

It was 14 years later before the Tour came back to the Palm Springs area in 1967. The one-day tournament was called the Seven Lakes Invitational. It was held at Seven Lakes Country Club which was an executive golf course, par 58. Mickey Wright shot seven under (51) and won it by two strokes. We played that tournament again the following year, and Sharon Miller won it.

A few weeks later, in November of 1968, Canyon Country Club hosted the Canyon Ladies Classic. Kathy Whitworth won that 54-hole tournament.

It would be four years before the Tour played in the Palm Springs area again, and that was the first Dinah Shore Tournament played at Mission Hills Country Club in 1972.

*1970s. Shirley and Marilynn Smith at the
Dinah Shore Golf Tournament.*

That tournament was the dream of one man, David Foster. His parents were Americans living in England, so David was born and raised in England. David became one of the most decorated pilots in the Royal Air Force in World War II. He was a hero in England. After the war, David worked his way up through the corporate ranks. He was president and later chairman of Colgate-Palmolive, a company his father had also held top positions.

David loved golf and wanted to promote his company's products to women. His idea was to have a ladies professional golf tournament the week before The Masters and to have it televised. He wanted a tournament that, like The Masters, played on the same course every year. First, he went to Florida to find a course. Since the week before The Masters usually falls near Easter, no resort was going to give up their course. That's a very busy week for golf courses in Florida, especially country clubs. He came out to the Palm Springs area and talked to Thunderbird, Indian Wells, Bermuda Dunes, and some others. Like Florida, none of them wanted to host it either.

Max Genet was an Oklahoma businessman. He bought property in Rancho Mirage just outside of Palm Springs. Max was building condos on his land in the early '70s and wanted to add a golf course but didn't have the capital. David talked to Max and said that he'd get Colgate-Palmolive to put up the money to build a course as long as they hosted his tournament each spring. Max agreed, and they built a course. They named it Mission Hills Country Club.

Colgate-Palmolive was a major sponsor of Dinah Shore's daytime talk show, *Dinah's Place*. David asked the famous singer/actress if they could use her name for this new tournament. She said "yes" thinking it was a tennis tournament since Dinah was an avid tennis player. When Dinah found out it was a golf tournament, she decided she better learn to play golf.

David wanted to get the tournament on TV, but ABC, NBC, and CBS didn't want it. He went to the Hughes Sports Network and convinced them to televise it. This first tournament in 1972 was called the Colgate-Dinah Shore Winners Circle Golf Championship. The last two holes on the final two days were televised to a national audience. That's how it started.

David dressed the caddies in white overalls which is the same gear they wear at The Masters. He copied The Masters as much as possible and yet kept in mind that his target audience was women.

Tour professionals had to have won, or finished second, or third in a tournament the year before to be eligible to play. That first year, 1972, they also invited all the club champions in the Palm Springs area to play in a pro-am format. My lifelong friend, Jane Woolley, was club champ at Indian Wells Country Club and got to play.

They hadn't had the chance to build the clubhouse yet at Mission Hills Country Club when they hosted that first Dinah. There was just a tent. The wind blew really hard that year, and some of the contestants complained. I don't know what they were expecting. They were in the desert, and sand blows here!

David never got enough credit for all he did. He really promoted women's golf and got the Tour on TV. Golf was the first major women's sport that Colgate-Palmolive sponsored, and because of David, the LPGA got national exposure.

A few years later, David retired from Colgate-Palmolive. The new president was a tennis fan. After 10 years, the new president decided that Colgate-Palmolive wouldn't sponsor the tournament any longer.

Thank goodness, RJR (Reynolds) Nabisco quickly stepped in

and kept it going. That was the 1982 tournament. They also kept Dinah as the host. Ross Johnson, the CEO of Nabisco, gave the tournament the shot in the arm it needed.

In 2000, Phillip-Morris bought Nabisco, which included the tournament, and they changed the name to the Kraft Nabisco Championship, dropping Dinah's name. That was sad to see. Old followers of the tournament still, and probably always will, call it the Dinah Shore. Phillip-Morris ran the tournament through 2014. All Nippon Airways (ANA) stepped up and took over the tournament in 2015.

Amy Alcott, a California girl, won The Dinah in 1988. It was her second time winning the tournament. After Amy won, she and her caddy celebrated the win by jumping into the lake which surrounds the 18th green. It took the gallery by surprise. Everyone loved it.

Juli Inkster won the following year and then Betsy King in 1990. Neither of them went for a swim.

Amy became the first three-time winner of the tournament in 1991. Dinah had told Amy that if she won and was going for a swim, she wanted to leap into the lake with her. Dinah always wore white slacks, but she had changed to black ones on that final day, so Amy knew Dinah was serious about wanting to jump.

The next leap wasn't until 1994 when Donna Andrews jumped in to honor Dinah, who had passed away just a month before the tournament. From then on, every winner has jumped or waded into the water. Pat Hurst can't swim, so she waded in after her win in 1998.

In 2006, in honor of the tournament's 35th anniversary, they built a pond and cemented it. They also closed it off from the rest of the lake so they could put chlorine in it like a swimming pool. Tournament officials didn't want the winner jumping into dirty lake water any longer. They wanted the water to be fresh. Terry Wilcox directed the tournament for 15 years. His grandchildren called him "Poppie," so they named it "Poppie's Pond" in Terry's honor. Over the years, jumping into the lake has become a tradition, much like the green jacket at The Masters.

David actually had Colgate sponsoring three ladies tournament for several years in the 1970s. They called it the Colgate Triple Crown. The Dinah was in the spring, the second tournament was in England in the summer, and the final tournament was in Melbourne, Australia in December. Players earned points by their finishing position in these three tournaments and then the top "x" number of players (this changed through the years) competed for the Colgate Triple Crown Trophy.

The Colgate Triple Crown finals started as 36 holes and grew to a 72-hole event. In its fourth year, it changed formats from stroke play to match play. The women competed for a purse which started at $50,000 and steadily grew to over $100,000 through the years. The winner also won a brand new car.

In 2008, during the Dinah, there was a reunion for LPGA

Tour players from the 1950s, 1960s, and 1970s. Susie McAllister Morton hosted a barbecue at her home. Susie played the Tour in the 70s and 80s. She had married Gary Morton, Lucille Ball's widower. Her home, on the 17th fairway of Thunderbird Country Club, was originally owned by Lucille Ball and Desi Arnaz. There was a tremendous turnout of players from the first three decades of the Tour. Several top amateur golfers, like Edean Ihlanfeldt, who helped us fill the field in the early days of the Tour, were also there.

I remember when David Foster walked in. He actually came to our reunion! There stood this little old gentleman, just shy of his 88th birthday. David was dressed to the nines. He had on a gold-buttoned, double-breasted blue suit coat. Utterly English! There were two young ladies, one on each side, helping him walk.

The dinner was outside, and all the pros were chatting. It suddenly got very quiet as people started to notice that David was standing on the patio. Then everyone started clapping, and David got a standing ovation from all the pros. We knew who he was! After he was seated, most of the older pros went over and chatted with him — Sandra Post, Kathy Whitworth, Judy Rankin, Marilynn Smith, Carol Mann, and the list goes on. Everyone knew he was the man who had done so much to put the Tour on the map by starting the Dinah Shore Tournament and getting it televised.

It was a wonderful evening with a great turnout. Women came from all over for this reunion — Chako (Hisako Higuchi) even flew in from Japan. So many of the pros I hadn't seen in years and years were there. We just don't have the chance to all get together very often. I can't remember a better evening than this!

The next day, H.B. Duntz MacArthur, who was married to James MacArthur of *Hawaii 5-0* fame, hosted a brunch at her home. This gave everyone another chance to catch up even more.

It was wonderful of Susie, H.B., and all those who helped them organize it, to give us "old" golf pros the chance to get together and reminisce. I'm sure it was a gathering most of us will never forget. I know I won't!

Along with great teaching abilities and understanding of the golf swing, Shirley's positive attitude and love of the game has added greatly to my joy of playing. Her instruction is always sprinkled with memorable stories of her life's experience as a member of the LPGA . . . designed to leave the student with a positive attitude and a sense of her love for the game of golf.

Alex Rocovitz
Student and Friend

Once upon a time, 13 women had a dream and formed the LPGA. That is what Shirely has done for me; made my golf dreams come true. Shirley has taught me to believe in myself, to never give up, and to be patient. She taught me that it's okay to not hit a perfect shot and most of all, to have fun.

I always learn something when I play golf with Shirley. She keeps things simple and understandable.

Shirley is very kind, caring, thoughtful, considerate, generous, supportive and loving, and has a great sense of humor. She is also a great Rummikub player.

She has made a huge impact in my life and I truly treasure her friendship. It's an honor to have Shirley as my friend. The time we spend together on and off the golf course is a treasure.

Love you so much Shirley!

Kathi Rocovitz
Student and Friend

HOLE # 11

Celebrities on the Course

The Palm Springs area is known for its desert beauty and became a relaxation destination for Hollywood celebrities beginning way back in the 1920s. While teaching at Tamarisk Country Club, Shirley worked with many famous people and developed friendships that would last a lifetime.

Bob and Delores Hope were both golfers. They lived in Toluca Lake, California, and were members of Lakeside Country Club. They also had a house in Palm Springs and were members of O'Donnell Golf Club. O'Donnell's was the only course when they first came to the desert.

William and Mousie Powell also played golf at O'Donnell, and Delores and Mousie were very close friends. Delores played a lot of golf with Mousie, and Mousie played a lot of golf with my dear friend Jane Woolley. Jane and Mousie played many amateur tournaments together.

Bob was an honorary member at Tamarisk and would come

1987. Shirley and friends at the Marilynn Smith Founder's Classic, Dallas, Texas. From left: Bettye Danoff, Alice Bauer, Marlene Bauer, Marilynn Smith, Shirley, Louise Suggs, Kathy Whitworth.

out to the course every once in a while. Delores also came over, and I would play with her. Bob was very involved with his tournament, the Bob Hope Desert Classic, and Delores had a soft spot in her heart for the LPGA.

Marilynn Smith asked Delores to come to the Founders Classic in Dallas, which was the first senior women's professional golf tournament. Delores actually went three years, from 1987 to 1989, and donated $10,000 each year to Marilynn's tournament. Delores later started a benevolent fund for LPGA pros who had played the

Tour. Retired pros could apply to the fund if they were experiencing a financial hardship. The Financial Assistance Fund was renamed the Delores Hope Fund after her generous donation of $1 million. It is still a vital part of the LPGA Foundation.

Mousie was also a life-long supporter of the LPGA. She initiated the "William and Mousie Powell Award" in 1986 in honor of her husband who had died two years earlier. William Powell was a well-known film star but had retired to Palm Springs by the mid-1950s. The award is given to the Tour player whose behavior and deeds best exemplify the spirit, ideals, and values of the LPGA. Kathy Whitworth received the first award which is voted on by all the Tour players.

At Tamarisk Country Club, I taught Danny Kaye, Kirk Douglas, Jack Benny, Milton Berle, Dean Martin, and the Marx Brothers.

Harpo Marx was my favorite. He used to try all kinds of crazy things. Harpo showed up one day with a piece of wood, and he said, "I'm going to stand strong on my left side." He carried this two-by-four with him all around the golf course. Every time he hit a shot, he would put the two-by-four down, put his foot on it, and lean onto his left side during his back swing. That was his thing for the day.

Harpo and I talked back and forth by whistling. He had a wig the color of my red hair. Once in a while, when we had a ladies tournament, Harpo and I would do a little skit.

Harpo and his wife, Susan, adopted four children. They built a house on several acres across from Tamarisk Country Club. They had the kids help design the house. Each of the four children had a say on what they wanted included. There was a garden, and they had several animals, including dogs and a horse. Each kid had jobs to help take care of everything.

Jane and I were invited to Harpo's home for dinner on many occasions. We ate at a round table with a huge lazy susan. We sat at the same place each time. When the food came around on the lazy susan, we helped ourselves.

Harpo was allowed one drink each night, so he had this glass that was pint-sized. That was his one drink. When he wanted us to go home, he would go and get his nightcap and put it on. He wouldn't say anything. You just knew it was time to leave.

Jack Benny was a student of Helen Dettweiler's at Thunderbird Country Club. Jack joined Tamarisk Country Club after it opened in 1952. I gave him playing lessons at Tamarisk. He would keep track of the time, glancing at his watch and saying, "I've got to go home in about 20 minutes. I have to practice."

I asked him, "What do you mean? Practice what?"

He said, "I practice the violin every day. I just come out here to relax." Jack was a very accomplished violinist. He would play it funny on TV but was actually a very good musician.

Jack would sit and have lunch with Milton Berle at the club. If I were walking through the dining room, he would say, "Come on over here and sit down, I want to introduce you. Milton," Jack would say, "this is my teacher, Shirley." So I would sit and eat lunch

*1960s. Kirk Douglas takes a lesson at
Tamarisk Country Club with Shirley.*

with them.

Once, while I was giving Jack a lesson, I told him that I had just found out my mother was very ill. She lived in Detroit, Michigan, and had developed diabetes.

"Well," he said, "we don't need to do this golf lesson. You should go home." Then he reached into his pocket and handed me some cash. He said, "Now you go and buy a ticket and see your mother." He was not a tightwad like people thought he was.

Walter Annenberg was also a very dear friend of mine. The Annenberg family owned all sorts of publications: the *Philadelphia Inquirer, TV Guide,* the *Daily Racing Form*, and *Seventeen* magazine. He was the ambassador to the United Kingdom for five-and-a-half years, from 1969 to 1974. The Annenbergs lived in Pennsylvania but came to the Palm Springs area in the winter to golf. He was a member of Tamarisk Country Club but decided to build his own course when Tamarisk became too busy, and he couldn't get a starting time. He bought the property next to Tamarisk in 1963. That's where Tamarisk had planned to build their main clubhouse and a second 18-hole golf course.

In 1964, Walter completed his 9-hole course, and in 1966 finished their home and moved in. They had quite an extensive art collection, and many famous people stayed there; including Frank Sinatra, Warren Buffett, Queen Elizabeth II, and eight U.S. presidents.

The Annenberg Estate was called Sunnylands. Walter named

it after a fishing camp his father had owned in the Poconos Mountains of Pennsylvania.

Once his course was finished, Walter could golf when he wanted and with whom he wanted. At the top of his backswing, Walter would loop the club before he started his downswing. I nicknamed him "Zorro" because of that. He was a very generous, kind-hearted man, and I was fortunate to have him as a friend.

I've played golf with countless LPGA and PGA professionals over the years, but I'll never forget playing with Arnold Palmer. I was teaching at Indian Wells Country Club, and Mr. Palmer was there to play a practice round before the start of the Bob Hope Desert Classic. He asked me to play with him. I couldn't believe it; I was so excited! I walked over to the starter shack with my clubs and the starter said, "You can't play today."

"Oh, yes I can," I answered. "Mr. Palmer asked me to play with him!"

After playing, Mr. Palmer was chatting with Shirley Englehorn and me. People approached us and wanted to take his picture. He told us, "Whenever someone takes your picture, be sure to take off your sunglasses, and always sign your name so someone can read it." I'll never forget that, though I don't know that I've always followed his advice.

Signatures of famous golfers as used on their pro-line golf clubs.

It has been an honor to get to know Shirley, as with all of the LPGA founders that I have met. I've always enjoyed chatting with Shirley, hearing all her stories and thoughts on the golf swing.

There are many things I admire about Shirley but one, in particular, is her passion to continue to learn and stay involved with the game! When she's at a LPGA event you will always find her on the range watching all the girls, getting to know them, and maybe even giving a tip or two. Also, you will find her chatting with the club reps and learning about all the technology and how it will help her game.

Shirley was and is a great teacher. Her love for the game is still very evident.

Karrie Webb
LPGA Tour Player
World Golf Hall of Fame

It was the love of the game that drove Shirley Spork to be one of 13 women who saw and believed in their future in the game of golf. In 1950, these women became the founding members of the Ladies Professional Golf Association, the LPGA.

But, her contribution to the game did not stop there, for deep down inside she was a teacher at heart. At a time when women's sports had a limited audience, Shirley knew that "growing the game" would depend on education.

Shirley never gave up on her dream. After countless hours of campaigning over several years, the LPGA Teaching Division was finally born in 1959. Her dream was to develop a program that provided the tools to teach women how to teach.

I was one of those eager players with teaching credentials who jumped on this opportunity. I'll never forget the wonderful, informative workshops for us "newbies" lead by Shirley Spork, Ellen Griffin, and Joanne Winter. They set the bar high, and I am forever grateful.

Shirley has been my friend and mentor for over 40 years — how lucky I have been to have her play that role in my life.

Thank you Shirley, for sharing your knowledge and wisdom and for all you continue to do for the game we love.

Pat Lange
LPGA Teaching & Club Professional - Master Life Member
LPGA Teaching & Club Professional - Hall of Fame

HOLE # 12

Tools of the Game

There are few sports which have experienced as many equipment changes as golf over the last 100 years. In her almost seven decades, Shirley has seen many of these trends come and go. From steel, to fiberglass, to graphite . . . Shirley's been there. From balata to Surlyn, Shirley's played them both. From blade to mallet, and then back to the blade. Many of the golf clubs amateurs enjoy today are a direct result of the collaboration between manufacturers and the early LPGA Tour players.

Back when golf started, there were only woods — spoons, brassies, and cleeks. The first golf club with an iron head was called a Rut Iron. The head was the width of a track made by a wagon wheel. If the ball rolled into a rut, you could use that club to hit it out. These were rare and expensive because they needed to be forged and pounded by a blacksmith.

When I came into the game, clubs were made with steel shafts, not wood. I didn't play with hickory. After steel came fiberglass shafts. To make a Golfcraft fiberglass shaft, they took a smooth steel rod and rolled it in Owens Corning fiberglass. Then they put it in an oven and heated it. The lighter the club, the faster you could swing it, and the farther you could hit the ball. It was the difference between a little buggy whip and a broom handle. This really changed the game.

The next advancement was an aluminum shaft from Spalding. It didn't sell well because it scratched and didn't look good. The aluminum also became brittle in cold weather, which caused it to break easily. They were around in the mid-'60s to the mid-'70s.

Then companies started working with aerospace engineers to test graphite — like they use in pencil lead. They took a gallon of glue and some graphite powder and formed it into a golf shaft. There were dozens of different qualities of graphite shafts. The more graphite they put in, the lighter it was, but the more it cost. The more glue, the cheaper and heavier the shaft.

All golf equipment companies had an advisory staff. Our job was to test their latest clubs. We would hit balls and tell them if the clubs were too light, too heavy, or whatever. After considering our input, they would decide whether or not to manufacture them for the public. The next step was to get the United States Golf Association's (USGA) approval. If the USGA okayed the club, then the manufacturers would include it in their line the following year.

All that went away when computer testing arrived on the scene. Computers took the place of people testing the equipment. Back in the day, at both the LPGA and PGA Tour stops, the manufacturers would bring their new stuff out for the pros to test. On Monday or Tuesday, most of the players would try the latest equipment. Then they would decide if they wanted to use it in a tournament. That's how the manufacturers got Tour player's endorsements.

Today, if you have 20 players all working for the same company, those 20 players may each be using a different shaft. This can be overwhelming for most amateur golfers. All the public really needs to know is the shaft flex (women's, men's, or senior) and the lie (upright, flat, or standard). They don't need all this extra information! Today, there are clubs with an adjustable screw head, and you can change it every which way to compensate for your mistakes. The average player never hits two balls the same anyway, so what difference does it make?

The biggest sellers are putters, drivers, and rescue clubs/hybrids. Golf shops these days analyze your swing on a machine. You pay them a hundred bucks, and they hand you a piece of paper telling you which club to buy. I don't need a computer to tell me what you're doing and what club you should be swinging.

Putting has changed over the years due to the texture of the greens. It seems that the greens are extremely fast these days. They run somewhere around 11 or 12 on the Stimpmeter. In the early days of the Tour, the greens would have probably registered more like an eight. Back then, we needed to take a bigger backswing which made controlling distance and direction much more challenging.

An old-fashioned putter would be difficult to use on the

new faster greens. Today, manufacturers are using various inserts to deaden the ball coming off the clubface to compensate for these fast greens. That's why many of the new putters are big and heavy. You just touch the ball, and it keeps rolling at a nice slow speed. You don't want the ball rolling too fast. You want it to go at an exacting speed as if a pendulum is swinging at the same speed every time. The ball has to roll like a wheel on a tire going over and over.

Your swing has to correspond with your putter of choice. If you use a blade putter with the shaft coming out of the back, you have to open and close it and swing it in a slight arc. A center-shafted putter moves more on a straight line like a pendulum and works from hooded to open.

When I first learned to play golf, the "stymie" was still part of competitive match play tournaments. At that time, a player wasn't required to mark their ball on the green. Your opponent would try and place their ball between your ball and the hole. If the balls were more than six inches apart, and the forward ball blocked the hole, the ball farthest away was considered "stymied." The player farthest away would have to putt around, or try and chip over, their opponent's ball that blocked the hole. Back in the day, scorecards were flat, not folded. They were exactly six inches long so you could use them to measure the distance between two balls on the green.

In 1938, the USGA added the rule that if the forward ball was within six inches of the hole, it was moved regardless of the distance between the two balls. They tested this for two years and then

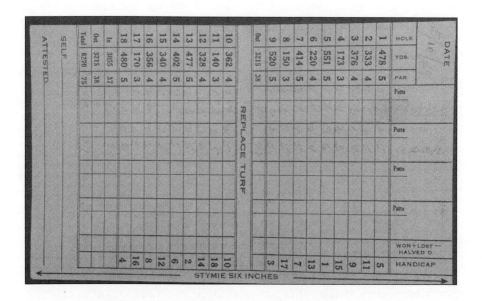

1949. A six-inch score card used to measure a stymie.

permanently added it to the rule book in 1942. The Stymie Rule was completely removed in 1952 when the USGA and the Royal and Ancient established their first set of joint rules. From then on, a ball on the green had to be marked if it was in the way. So, I've played it both ways in my career.

In my opinion, choosing a sand wedge is also confusing for the average golfer — there are way too many of them. They're available in lofts of 52, 54, 56, 58, 60, 62, and so on. Many players today have several wedges in their bag. Once I looked in Betsy King's bag, and she had three wedges. I asked, "What are these for?"

"Well, this one goes this far, that goes that far, and the other one goes that far," Betsy said. She had a club for each distance. Car-

247

rying several wedges makes sense for Tour players who hit the ball consistently, but the average player wouldn't hit a wedge the same distance twice in a round.

We had one or two wedges, and we made all the shots with those clubs. Equipment has really changed the game.

Golf balls have not changed much in the last ten years, and like clubs, they test them on a computer. Manufacturers can regulate the number, size, and shape of the dimples. That affects how high the ball flies and how it responds on short shots around the greens.

If you go to the grocery store to buy some soda pop, you see that Coca-Cola makes diet, regular, two or three flavors, caffeine, and non-caffeine. That gets the soda company a lot of shelf space which is good advertising. Titleist makes several varieties of golf balls and, like the soda companies, gets lots of shelf space. People go to the golf store looking to buy a golf ball, and they have all these choices. They spend all this time wondering which one they should buy. The salesperson is supposed to ask, "What's your club head speed? Do you want to hit it high or low?" Most of the time, it doesn't make any difference since the majority of golfers don't hit the ball the same way twice. Plus, they're just as likely to hit their brand new ball out of bounds or dunk it in a water hazard. The salesperson should tell them to pick a ball that's on sale. Just buy the least expensive one, but of course, they can't say that.

It doesn't cost a lot of money to make a golf ball — like less than 30 cents. What increases the price is the advertising, packaging, and shipping. Big companies can absorb these extra costs, but that's tough for small companies that don't make several different types of golf balls.

Golf balls used to be made in different windings — they were wound with rubber. The tighter the rubber was wound and the more rubber used, the harder you had to hit it to make it expand. They were made in 90 and 100 compressions. Later, ball manufacturers took one and wound it looser, at 80 compression, so that Little Miss Muffet could poof it out there 100 yards.

Today, to sell balls, they make a large variety — you can purchase a solid ball, or one that has two, three, or four pieces. They also have different kinds of covers and different dimple patterns.

When I endorsed and used Penfold golf balls, I had the opportunity to take a tour through their factory. One lady sat there by a machine all day and watched the rubber thread wind. Then she passed it down to the next lady who put the cover on it. It was very interesting to watch.

When I was working with the National Golf Foundation (NGF), a chemical company first introduced the "solid ball." They made it in different compressions. They wanted to know how to distribute it in the market. The key was to get a company that made clubs to endorse the ball. Next, you needed to get Tour players to use it and endorse it. That's how you got exposure so people would know about it and buy it. The inventor, Princeton Chemical Company, didn't have enough money to spend on advertising, so they floundered around for a few years and finally in 1967 sold their patent to Spalding.

Spalding then made all their range balls from this patent. They were cheap to make because they were just one piece. A golfer could buy the same ball that was used on the driving range in the pro shop. Spalding put a different name on it and sold it for a higher price than the range ball.

Some golf balls were made in two pieces, and the procedure was called the Geer Patent Cover. It's like taking a muffin pan. You set a piece of balata in it. Then you put in the core. The top of the mold was another piece of balata. Then the top of the machine came down, and the heat compressed it together.

Titleist made a seamed ball and then came a solid one-piece ball. And now we have all these other types, with everyone trying to sell something different.

Golf ball covers used to be softer and were called balata. They were made from sap that came from balata trees found in the Caribbean, and Central and South America. If you miss-hit it, you would put a cut in it. Golfers called it a "smile," and it actually looked like one.

DuPont came up with a substance in the 1960s that wouldn't cut called Surlyn. Golf ball companies guarantee to replace balls that were cut. They didn't have to replace many because players would lose them before they ever cut them.

Ping started making golf balls after buying the molds and the rights to certain models from Titleist. They made two-colored golf balls – one color on each side. Ping gave these two-colored balls to golf pros for use in their junior programs. Some of the color combinations have become collector's items because so few were made.

When I was playing the Tour, I could tell the difference in balls. If I was blindfolded and putted a Titleist, MacGregor, or Spalding ball, I could tell you which one it was just by the touch and feel in my hand. I can't do that today because there are way too many varying components.

Not too many pros today have the same kind of endorsement contracts that we had. It used to be if you used certain equipment, your company would either match what you won in a tournament or even send you a little extra. It was good advertising for them if you won a tournament using their equipment.

Today, the players have brand names all over their hats, clothes, and golf bags. Companies know what receives more TV coverage and pay accordingly. A player's hat and back of the collar receive more air time than their shoes, and the left sleeve is more valuable than the right sleeve. It's about visibilty. How often a company's logo is seen on TV. Fees are also tied into how competitive a player is. Being in contention leads to more TV exposure, which companies love.

A lot of people love to wear big-name fashions, but not me. I never wanted to buy clothes with a brand name showing on it. When I worked at Tamarisk Country Club, I would come home and say to my housemate, Jane Woolley, "All those women have the same kind of purse."

Jane would ask, "What color is it?"

"Brown and tan," I answered.

"It's a Gucci," Jane explained.

Then I'd say, "I think it's dumb! It looks like they all played in the same tournament and got the purse as a tee prize."

All you really need to play the game today is a few golf clubs. Make sure the shafts match your swing speed and the grip is the correct size for your hand. Grab some tees and some golf balls that are on sale. Then find a LPGA Teaching Professional you can understand and communicate with, and take lots of lessons. You learn to play the game of golf out on the course, but you can't play the game of golf if you can't hit the ball! And you learn to hit the ball with the help of a pro at the driving range, not on the course.

What a MARVELOUS teacher! Wanting to be a better golfer, friends suggested I take a lesson from their favorite teacher, Shirley Spork. How fortunate I was to be guided by her expertise. What a gem!

Drills, practice, and "Sporkisms" like "Shir-ley-SPORK!" More than a teacher, Shirley has become my mentor and role model. I keep learning each and every time we are together. Her knowledge and fun history lessons are special.

Shirley has taught golf for nearly seven decades and her students keep coming back. They continue to improve with Shirley's constant guidance.

Shirley is a teacher's teacher. She's the very best on and off the golf course.

Tina Barker
Student and Friend

HOLE # 13

Collections

You would expect a golf professional to have collected golf clubs over the years, but ducks? Ducks would probably not make the top 10 on most lists. It's interesting to hear what and why people have collections. Shirley's lifelong "affair" with ducks spans over seven decades. Most of the states across the nation are represented in her collection, as well as many countries throughout the world.

Ducks have played an important part of my life since I was very young. My family started raising mallards, along with chickens and rabbits, when I was 12 years old. We moved from Detroit to our property that ran along the 17th hole of the Bonnie Brook Golf Course on the outskirts of the city.

We raised ducks for their eggs. They have large yolks which make great scrambled eggs. Every so often we woud also have duck for dinner. I did not enjoy dressing them, trying to pull out all the pin feathers, but I did love their choice dark meat.

As I progressed down life's fairways, my next venture was

raising my own ducks. I won four baby ducks at the Mendocino County Fair. This was when I was got my first head pro job at Ukiah Municipal Golf Course in Ukiah, California, in 1952. I named each one, painting their initials on their bills with nail polish: H - Hook, S - Slice, T - Top, P - Par. They were my alarm system as I lived alone near the clubhouse and the 9th green. If there was any night activity, they would warn me. Some people have dogs; I had ducks.

During the past 67-plus years of traveling, I've amassed a large duck collection. I have well over 200 — made from all sorts of materials from soap to gold and everything in between.

I purchased a solid-gold miniature duck on the Ponte Vecchio Bridge in Florence, Italy. Then there's the soapstone duck from Alaska and the Petoskey stone from Michigan. I have one made out of a reed from Italy and some beautiful, old duck decoys from my time in Vermont. I have a china soup tureen in the shape of a duck, and a duck wind chime in my backyard.

Many of my close friends have added to my collection over the years. I have a duck hairdryer from my lifelong friend and housemate, Jane Woolley. There is duck wallpaper in my bathroom and a duck soap dispenser next to the sink.

I have a duck telephone from my dear friend, the late Mousie Powell. It quacks when it rings. The ringtone on my cell phone is also a duck quack.

It is fun to reminisce and tell the stories of where, what, and when I collected some of these treasures. I have also carved some

1980. Patty Berg admiring some of Shirley's antique golf clubs on Easter Sunday at Shirley's home in Palm Desert.

ducks and given them away as gifts to my friends.

I also have a quite a collection of antique golf clubs. I already mentioned the A. Patrick Long Nose club that I received as a gift from Mr. Wilson after playing with him at St Andrews in 1951. It dates back to the 1870s and is one of the most highly-treasured clubs in my collection. I also have one of the early irons used in golf, called a Rut Club.

I have some Fancy Face hickory-shafted woods and a Walter Hagen sand iron. The sand iron, known as a Sandy Andy, was manufactured by the L.A. Young Company of Detroit, Michigan, starting in 1928. It has a large, concaved, smooth face; a large flange in the back, a wooden shaft, and a leather grip. They were quickly banished by the PGA Tour, so they were only in production for two years. I have a large collection, but these are some of my favorites.

When Jane and I lived together, we always had dogs. We would have two at a time — a Westie and a Scottie. They were always female and named after European royalty like Tammy and Annie Lorie.

Because of our pets, I have a large Sherratt & Simpson figurine collection. Sherratt & Simpson was an English company that produced figurines of a wide array of animals. I have several Westie and Scottie figurines in my collection.

Bag tags are another one of my collections. I have tags from all over the world — everywhere I worked, played, taught, attended a tournament, or was invited to a conference. If there was a bag tag, I made sure to get one. Now they are all tacked to the walls surrounding my bar. It's fun to look at them and reminisce while I'm fixing my evening cocktail . . . they bring back so many fond memories.

A few of the hundreds of bag tags in Shirley's collections.

More of Shirley's bag tag collection

I met Shirley while attending LPGA meetings and educational seminars. I was surprised at her questions until I realized that was her way of encouraging discussions and helping us learn about our profession.

When I went for my Class "A" rating, Shirley was one of my evaluators. I was nervous, but she immediately made me feel comfortable. Later in my career I became an evaluator and the memory of Shirley's professionalism helped me so much. Having Shirley leading our evaluation team enhanced the process for all of us.

I became a member of Shirley's teaching staff at The School of Golf. I have fond memories of our trips together from Palm Desert to San Diego. There I learned more about the love and dedication Shirley has for all aspects of her profession; playing, teaching, and sharing wonderful stories of her experiences through the years.

I will always cherish the ways she inspired and motivated me to be the best I could be. I know countless others who have benefited from having Shirley Spork in some part of their world.

Doris J Earls
LPGA Teaching & Club Professional - Master Life Member

A definite LIKE! Shirley on a thrilling tour of the desert,
Palm Springs, and the Coachella Valley.
A bird's-eye view of her home and the 100-plus golf courses in the area.

HOLE # 14

Likes and Dislikes

Everyone has likes and dislikes and Shirley is no different. Here are a few of the items that made her list.

LIKES	DISLIKES
GOLF	

LIKES	DISLIKES
Links-style courses	Holes with no layup areas
Flexible, Ultra-Lite graphite golf shafts	Stiff steel shafts
Small greens	Large, undulating greens
Par-3 holes	Long, uphill par-5 holes
Short-game shots – ¼, ½, ¾	Long fairway shots, thick rough
Clean, firm-fitting shoes & gloves	Visors & baseball caps
Course beauty: trees, flowers	Players who talk, walk in your line & play slow

LIKES	DISLIKES

FOOD

LIKES	DISLIKES
My mother's fried chicken	Hot, spicy foods
Rhubarb pie	Sweet soft puddings
Wok dinners	Over-cooked meat
Roasted fowl & beef	Rutabagas
Soft cookies	Blanched vegetables
Dry cereals	Over-cooked eggs
Hearty, thick vegetable soup	Warm milk

CLOTHES

LIKES	DISLIKES
Business attire, pants suits	Fancy, fashion designer cocktail dresses
Tailored, matching-fashion sports clothes	High heel shoes
Large-rimmed, sun-protection golf hats	Flip flops
Small purses	Large, designer purses
Sun lotion protection	Sleeveless blouses
Favorite colors: dark brown, navy, greens, yellows	Big flowery prints or polka dots

Shirley Geraldine Spork and I have been dear friends for 27 years. She has so many great friends because she is such a wonderful and thoughtful friend! We have laughed, traveled, golfed, worshiped, dined, consoled, and supported each other. We chat nearly every other day. She has been my friend, coach, mentor, and my "other mother."

But my favorite story is of our first 10 minutes together. As a brand new golfer, I showed up for my first golf lesson. I knew Shirley was tough. I had been told that she "eats bad golfers for breakfast" and that she actually refuses to teach golfers who won't practice. She asked what I wanted to work on. Huh? I must have read an article about the weight shift in the swing because I replied, "I think I need to work on my weight shift."

"Fine," she said, "let's see you hit a few balls." It wasn't long before she stopped me and said, "You don't have any trouble with your weight shift. You don't have one." I knew then that I loved her because she was honest with me, and always has been.

Within five years of that lesson, I won my first club championship. Shirley called me every night during the tournament and coached me over the phone. After thanking my mother in my acceptance speech, Shirley was my next accolade!

Shirley has mellowed a lot over the years, but her dedication to growing the game, especially for women, remains unchanged.

She has never forgotten anyone she has met, or anything she has ever seen, or heard, or done, or learned. She is seriously curious.

No grass grows under her feet. She never shows up on your doorstep empty-handed. And she has taught me so very much more than golf.

I love you Spooky, and I don't know anyone who doesn't!

Sandy Fenton

Student and Friend

HOLE # 15

Firsts

In addition to the countless award and accolades Shirley has received over the years, she has notched a significant number of "firsts." These aren't found in the record books, but they likely opened doors for the women who followed.

First LPGA Woman Professional to manage three golf facilities:
1951 - Ukiah Municipal Golf Course, Ukiah, California
1959 - Tanforan Golf Course, San Bruno, California
1964 - Sugarbush Golf Course, Warren, Vermont

1951 - First American Female Golf Professional admitted into the Royal & Ancient Clubhouse at St Andrews (including the board room and men's locker room/smoker area). *Interesting note: Babe Zaharias won the Women's British Amateur in 1947 at Gullane Golf Club in Scotland. After her historic win, Babe was interviewed by the press on the steps of St Andrews, but she wasn't allowed in the clubhouse. So, look at the difference four short years made as I walked through the front door and another barrier was broken down.*

1951 - Gave numerous exhibitions in England, Wales, France for A.E. Penfold Golf Ball Company. *At the end of each exhibition, I collected money on the 18th green for local junior golf programs.*

1952 - Only LPGA Professional invited to play in The Northern California - Reno Open, a PGA event.

1952 - First to have Foot Joy design a pair of shoes that were green/white. *Prior to this, Foot Joy only made shoes that were black, white, brown, brown/white, or black/white.*

1952 - First to design a powder-blue/gold-fleck, glass golf club shaft for my sponsor Golfcraft. *I used these for exhibitions and tournaments.*

1960 - First LPGA professional to be invited to be a guest speaker (along with Harvey Penick) at the men's PGA National Meeting in Scottsdale, Arizona.

1960 - First to give a National Golf Foundation (NGF) workshop/clinic for the California Physical Education Teacher's Conference, in Big Bear Lake, CA. *We hit whiffle balls off of carpet samples on the side hill of a slanted parking lot.*

My earliest memory of Shirley is what I read when researching women's golf history. I was thrilled when I met Shirley through mutual friends. They casually mentioned that Shirley was their coach. I said, "The Shirley Spork? One of the founders of the LPGA?" I begged for them to introduce me to her, they did, and we became fast friends.

I am a senior golfer and Shirley has patiently taken me through a series of lessons over the past three years. One of her frequent sayings is that all golfers are not alike and a teacher needs to craft her teaching to fit the individual. She told me she has laid awake at night coming up with a lesson that would teach me the concept I was struggling with.

Feel is the hardest concept for me. I have hit plastic golf balls onto Shirley's roof and into the neighbor's yard while practicing pitching with a beach ball between my legs! She has made me hit balls with my hands taped together around the club to make sure my grip was correct. I have swung a club filled with water sloshing to find transition. She has great imagination for teaching aids and they work. This year I was fortunate to become our club champion thanks to Shirley!

Shirley has generously introduced me to her circle of friends and to the LPGA family. Her balance in life has created a role model for me. Her faith is present in her daily life and she is known to cook and deliver meals to those who can't get out of their homes. She follows her collegiate sports teams, the horse races, and never misses a book sale. Did I mention she was a good cook?

Shirley is also quite a comedian. Many of her students can laugh when they recall a swing key like, "Don't be a one-eyed chicken!"

A very special moment for me was the 2015 Marilynn Smith LPGA Charity Pro-Am Tournament in Goodyear, Arizona. Shirley and Marilynn shared their memories with the LPGA Pros and guests. The film crew of the "Founders Film" was there and followed our team around the golf course and then on for a Pink Jeep ride. Shirley was thrilled to take our team on this ride through Sedona's beautiful valley.

I count my blessings to have Shirley Geraldine, "Spooky Duke," Spork as my coach, pro, teacher, and friend. I can't wait to read her book!

Pj Lowrey
Student and Friend

HOLE # 16

"Spork-isms"

Each person creates a unique language . . . words that take on a meaning of their own. Shirley is no exception. Welcome to the world of "SPORK-ISMS!" Throughout her teaching life, she has coined phrases that speak to her students. Phrases that create a picture for those who are learning to play the game which has been the focus of Shirley's life. This amazing game called golf.

FULL SWING PHRASES:
1. Waggle – Set – Swing

    Keep yourself loose and relaxed. Get quiet for a moment, gather yourself. Then swing the club.

2. Ball – Ball – Divot

    Hit the ball first. Take a divot **after** the ball.

3. Less is more! Use only 70% of your effort.

    You can't control 100% effort. You want a swing that's repeatable.

4. Shir – ley – SPORK

> The backswing should be slow and controlled.
>
> Shir – ley is the cadence for the backswing.
>
> SPORK is the pace of the downswing which is
> bold and free.

5. Finish what you start

> Follow through to a complete, balanced finish.

6. Finish like a star

> In balance, like you're having your picture taken.

7. Set – Turn – Release

> Set the club. Turn your body back. Release the club through
> to a finish.

8. Apple the pie and a coffee

> "A-p-p-l-e t-h-e p-i-e" is the tempo of the backswing.
>
> "And-a-coffee" is the speed of the downswing.

9. Sit Down – Stay Down – Go Down

> Sit down into your set up. Stay down on your backswing.
>
> Use your legs to go down after the ball on the downswing.

10. See it – Feel it – Trust it

>See the shot you are setting up to hit. Feel your swing.
>Then let go of all the thinking and trust your mechanics.

11. Back – Back – Forward

>Use this tempo for your full swing. Take the time to finish
>your backswing before starting your downswing. The best
>golfers I've ever seen were patient. They take the time to
>finish the backswing.

12. Hold your finish on full swings until the ball lands.

>Balance is of utmost importance for a good, repeatable golf
>swing.

CHIPPING/PITCHING PHRASES:

1. Triangle – Track – Target

>Arms and shoulders create a triangle. Club head swings on a
>track. Finish facing the target.

2. Hold your finish on chip and pitch shots until the ball
   stops rolling.

PUTTING PHRASES:

1. Stop – Look – Listen

> Stop moving. Look at the ball.
>
> Listen for the ball to drop into the hole.

2. Low – And – Slow

> Keep the putter low and swing it back slowly.

3. Fast Green Speeds

> Think of the ball as a raw egg – don't crack it.
>
> Hold the club – don't grip it!
>
> As you take the putter back, feel like you're pulling it through molasses.
>
> LOW – AND – SLOW

4. Judging the Distance

> Based on a level putt, count the paces using your normal gait from the ball to the cup. Each pace equals approximately one inch the putter head should move on the backswing.

5. Grip Pressure

    Scale of 1 to 10 (1 = very light, 10 = very firm)

Green	Stimpmeter	Pressure
Wet	8	8 - 10
Dry	10	5 – 6
Dry	11+	3 – 4

6. Length of Putts

    Long Putts (30-plus feet) – hold the putter at the top of the grip

    Medium Putts (6 to 15 feet) – hold the putter in the middle of the grip

    Short Putts (1 to 5 feet) – hold the putter at the bottom of the grip

7. There are three partial swings:

    Chip = 1/4 swing – hands swing knee to knee

    Small Pitch/Sand = 1/2 swing – hands swing hip to hip

    Big Pitch = 3/4 swing – hands swing shoulder to shoulder

Wanting to play well is a goal which takes correct, repetitive practice routines with guidance from your LPGA coach and/or teacher. Practice doesn't make perfect, it makes permanent. Only perfect practice makes perfect! If you're practicing your mistakes,

1960's. Shirley shares "Spork-isms" with a young student.

you're wasting your time and money.

When hitting over a problem area, (such as water, a ravine, or sand) use the club in which you have the most confidence. You can grip up or down on this club for different distances.

In order to score on the golf course, you must have a club that you can hit 50 yards, 100 yards, and 100-plus yards. It also helps to be good on and around the greens.

We play golf with our eyes, our hands, and our feet. The eyes tell us what direction and how far we have to go. Our hands hold onto and guide the club. Our feet deliver the power and the path of the club head.

Shirley Spork's legacy in the golf industry is an amazing story that is filled with passion, grit, perseverance, hard work, dedication, and an uncanny intelligence. These traits are reflective of an incredible lady, but the one that stands alone is "LOVE."

Shirley's love of the game and all the gifts the game bestows are evident when you are in her presence. Her passion and love for sharing this incredible game, and her tireless dedication to the sport, combined with her willingness to mentor other professionals, have changed countless lives for decades.

As a founding member, Shirley was significant in launching the LPGA Tour, yet I believe her greatest contribution to the game of golf was her early recognition for the need of an educational program to develop future golf instructors. Developing and writing early curriculum provided the foundation for today's LPGA Teaching & Club Professional Division. The immense undertaking was difficult and challenging but Shirley, being Shirley, approached the daunting task; first with an unflappable belief in the critical need for quality instruction, and second with the same analogy as how one would go about eating an elephant — one bite at a time! Many a frustrated or impatient student has heard her explain that that is the ONLY way to eat an elephant. It may take a while but slow and steady will get the job done.

Shirley doesn't just "talk the talk," she "walks the walk." Her selfless devotion of time and knowledge which she has shared with the golf world over the years is immeasurable. Each golf professional and player in the game owes Shirley a debt of gratitude for being an early pioneer and remarkable steward of this great game we call golf.

I am incredibly honored to call her my mentor and friend. Shirley, you are truly my diamond in the rough!

Forever in your debt —

Diane McHeffey
LPGA Teaching & Club Professional - Class "A" Member
PGA - Class "A" Member

I was honored when Shirley asked me to write a letter for her book. I have been her student and friend for 57 years. I first saw Shirley when she gave a clinic in 1960 at California Country Club. After the clinic I asked her if I could take a lesson.

As we started working together more I would stay at Shirley's house for three or four days. I took lessons, hit balls, and play some holes with her when she finished her other lessons. At the end of the day, we would go to her home where she would cook dinner, and I would hit balls into a net in her back yard under a light. The golf swing I learned from Shirley has stood the test of time.

While on the LPGA Tour, Shirley and Patty Berg would go to Mass every week. Sometimes on Sunday in Palm Springs, our foursome would go to Mass with her. The priest often still had his golf shoes on when he knelt at the altar. He would make sure to tell us to put all our golf winnings in the collection plate since he had seen us playing on the course.

Over the years, I had heard many stories from Shirley about the LPGA Tour and the LPGA Teaching Division. Because of that, I joined the LPGA and became both a Class "A" Tour Player and a Class "A" Teaching Professional.

Every time we are together I learn more about Shirley and the LPGA. I met Arnold Palmer because of Shirley. Shirley is always helping all levels of golfers with their games.

I love the fact that, at 90 years of age, she is still playing this great game, and I hope to be able to do the same. She still has an enviable short game.

The golf world owes a big thanks to Shirley and the other LPGA founders for their dedication to and love for the game of golf.

Carla J. Glasgow
LPGA Tour - Life Member
LPGA Teaching & Club Professional - Class "A" Member

HOLE # 17

Employment Facilities

During the past six decades Shirley has been affiliated as a golf professional and/or manager at the following courses:

1. Pasatiempo Golf Club - Santa Cruz, California
2. Ukiah Municipal Golf Course - Ukiah, California
3. Fox Hills Country Club - Culver City, California
4. Tamarisk Country Club - Rancho Mirage, California
5. Northmoor Country Club - Highland Park, Illinois
6. Sunset Ridge Country Club - Glenview, Illinois
7. Tanforan Golf Course - San Bruno, California
8. Sugarbush Golf Course - Warren, Vermont
9. Indian Wells Country Club - Indian Wells, California
10. Monterey Country Cluib - Palm Desert, California
11. Whispering Palms Country Club (renamed Morgan Run Club & Resort) - Rancho Santa Fe, California (The School of Golf for Women Only)
12. Singing Hills Golf Course (renamed Sycuan Golf Resort) - El Cajon, California (The School of Golf for Women Only)

13. Payson Golf Course - Payson, Arizona (Diamonds in the Rough Golf School)

Throughout Shirley's career she continued to work on her game.

The first time I met Shirley, she asked me a simple but very pointed question, "What are you personally doing to leave the game better?" I realized right then what made Shirley (and each of the LPGA founders) so special. They consistently focused on enhancing opportunities for women - not only for themselves but for the young girls who would follow.

At the LPGA, we have a motto that says, "Act Like a Founder." It is a personal challenge to every employee, player, and teacher in our organization that they be committed to leaving the game better than they found it. Shirley has always lived that motto, and now we try to follow her lead.

Shirley Spork didn't just play golf. Shirley Spork didn't just teach golf. Shirley Spork made golf a better place for women. And in doing so, she made the game better in every way!

Mike Whan
LPGA Commissioner

Shirley supporting her alma mater,
Eastern Michigan University.

HOLE # 18

Accomplishments and Awards

Shirley's life has incorporated various aspects of this game we call golf . . . from playing, to running golf facilities, to working for the National Golf Foundation (NGF), to teaching, to running golf schools, to serving on various committees. The list is endless and so are the awards she has received throughout the seven decades of her commitment to the great sport of golf. Here are just a few of the highlights.

1946, 1947, 1949 - Champion, Detroit District Golf Stroke-Play

1946 - Runner Up, Detroit District Golf Match-Play

1947 - Champion, Women's National Collegiate Golf

1947, 1948 - Champion, Detroit District Golf Match-Play

1947, 1948 - Runner Up, Michigan State Amateur

1948 - Runner Up, Detroit District Golf Stroke-Play

1948 - Amateur Champion, Tam O'Shanter All-American

1949 - Champion, Michigan State Amateur

1950-1968 - Advisory Staff Member, Golfcraft

1950 - Faculty Member, Bowling Green State University

1950 - Founding Member, LPGA Tour

1953, 1954 - Head Professional/Manager, Ukiah Municipal Golf
  Course

1959 - Founding Member, LPGA Teaching Division

1959 - Champion, California Derby Open (aka The California
  Women's Medal Golf Championship)

1959, 1984 - LPGA National Teacher of the Year

1960-1967 - Co-Chair, LPGA National Golf School

1961, 1962 - Head Professional/Manager, Tanforan Golf Course

1962 - Runner Up, LPGA Championship

1964, 1965 - Head Professional/Manager, Sugarbush Golf Course

1966-1973 - Western Educational Director, National Golf
  Foundation (NGF)

1968 - Recipient, Shirley Englehorn Award

1969 - Certificate of Appreciation, California Coaches Association

1970s - Co-owner, Diamonds in the Rough Golf Schools, Payson,
  Arizona

1973, 1974 - Recipient, Bob Hope Desert Classic Award

1976 - Recipient, Joe Graffis Award

1977-2002 - Director of Instruction, The School of Golf for
  Women Only

1981 - First Woman Inductee, Eastern Michigan University
  Athletic Hall of Fame

1989 - Recipient, Marilynn Smith Award

1989 - Recipient, Meritorious Service Award, Excel Charities

1994 - Recipient, Intercollegiate Golf Merit Award

1994 - Recipient, Byron Nelson Award

1998 - Recipient, LPGA Ellen Griffin Rolex Award

2000 - Inductee, LPGA Teaching and Club Professional (T&CP) Hall of Fame Inaugural Class

2000 - Recipient, LPGA Commissioner's Award

2001 - Recipient, Leadership Award, Executive Women's Golf Association (EWGA)

2002 - Recipient, Alumni Award, Redford High School, Detroit, Michigan

2002 - Inductee, Michigan Golf Hall of Fame

2003 - Honoree, Minerva Foundation of British Columbia

2007 - Recipient, Ginn Tribute (hosted by Annika Sörenstam)

2014 - Recipient, Lifetime Achievement Award, Michigan Women's Golf Association

2014 - Recipient, Varsity Letter "E," Eastern Michigan University (belated award for being National Collegiate Golf Champion in 1947)

2015 - Recipient, LPGA Patty Berg Award

1951. Shirley Spork woods and irons by Golfcraft.
Advertisement in Professional Golfer Magazine.

Epilogue

It all began with a putter. A putter! Purchased by a little red-haired girl with money she had earned selling soda pop, candy, and golf balls she had found on the property where she grew up — property that ran along the 17th fairway of the Bonnie Brook Golf Course in Detroit, Michigan. What a lifetime of experiences the game of golf has provided starting way back in the 1930s.

Shirley Spork has done everything the game of golf has to offer: mastering the various shots, building golf courses, managing golf properties, organizing teaching events, running tournaments, and teaching people from all walks of life.

Perhaps most important is not the stories, but the connections. Connections, not only with the game which she has played for nearly eight decades, but with the people Shirley has had the opportunity to meet, to know, and to love.

Through the years I have met a lot of people and made many dear friends. It was fun to go to work every day and teach because people who came to me wanted to learn how to play. A lot of golfers today want instant success, and there is no instant success in golf! You can buy a set of golf clubs and take six lessons, but that's not the answer. It takes a person years to understand what they're trying to do and the rest of their life to do it! It's just not an easy game!!!

Learning to play the game of golf is like eating an elephant. It's overwhelming unless you eat just one bite at a time and slowly digest it. I have played golf for almost 80 years, and in my life, I have eaten probably six-eighths of the elephant. Hopefully, I'll have time to work on that one next bite.

Shirley and her beloved friend, ParTee.

About the Authors

Nancy Bannon

I met Shirley not long after joining the LPGA Teaching Division. It was December of 1982 in El Cajon, California. Singing Hills Golf Course, now known as Sycuan Golf Resort, was hosting our first LPGA National Teaching Seminar. Who could have guessed that a few years later I would return to Singing Hills as an instructor at Shirley's golf school: The School of Golf for Women Only.

I had just transferred from the Central to the Western Section and had no idea who Shirley Spork was, other than one of the conference speakers. Over the next couple of days, it became painfully obvious to me that I was one of only a handful who was clueless. Well, that has certainly changed over the past 34 years.

I've had the privilege of being taught by, and have taught with, one of the greatest teachers the game has ever and probably will ever know. I am a Class "A" Life Member of the LPGA and have worked with people learning this wonderful game since 1980. Over the years, my students have grown tired of hearing me say, "Well,

Shirley would say . . ." or "My coach told me . . ." Shirley has been my greatest mentor, as she has to so many others.

Over the years, I have been blessed to hear story after story about the early days of the Tour. Every time Shirley told a story, someone in the group would say, "You have to write that down before it's too late." Well, I'm glad we didn't wait until it was "too late."

I have a journalism degree so was the "logical" choice to record these timeless tales. But let me tell you, writing a book, because you were a journalism major (like 35-plus years ago), is about as big a leap as becoming a Tour professional because you sunk a straight, uphill, 20-foot putt during a scramble tournament. Quite a stretch!!!

Without my dear friend and fellow journalism major, Connie Kuber, I have no doubt that it would have never seen the printed page. But, after countless interviews and exhaustive fact checking, here it is.

This project has been years in the making — way too many if you ask Shirley. But, God's timing is **always** perfect!

I wish you had the opportunity to sit in Shirley's backyard or at her dining room table and just listen to her talk. No one tells a story like Shirley. The printed word is a far cry from being there in person, but for those of you who won't have the privilege of meeting Shirley, hopefully, we've captured a tiny bit of her remarkable life for you to enjoy.

A heartfelt thank you to all who have contributed to this project and to my mentor and friend, Shirley Spork, for allowing me the honor of preserving some of her stories for generations of golfers to come.

Connie Kuber

My first stories were written in pencil on wide-ruled paper and told of the cows, horses, and dogs I grew up with. As a Minnesota dairy farmer's daughter, I have a passion for agriculture and the people who feed the world.

My professional career has included marketing cattle genetics throughout the world, writing for agricultural trade journals, and for the past 20 years, owning Connor Agriscience, an agriculture education and marketing company, with my husband, Ron.

Thank you to my children: Catharine, her husband Kyle, my son, Christopher, and my daughter, Madeline for your unwavering support. Thank you to my Ron, who always believes in me and in us. Thank you to God for always being there and always being good.

I hope that these written stories of Shirley's life experiences paint as vivid a picture in your mind as they do when she tells them in person.

I believe everyone has a story to tell and that documenting those stories is a gift to be shared. I encourage you to jot down a few memories in a notebook, speak them into a recorder, or tell them to someone else. Your story is important. It has been my pleasure to be part of sharing Shirley's.

Made in the USA
Middletown, DE
13 April 2019